Successful Insight *through* Prophetic Revelations

Understanding the Ministry of Prophecy

Dr. Michael L. Mosley

Successful Insight through Prophetic Revelations

Cover Design: Forbes Design

Cover Photo: Kenneth Grissom

Copyright © 2019

ALL RIGHTS RESERVED. No part of this work covered by the copyright herein may be reproduced, transmitted, stored or used in any form or by any means of graphic, electronic, or mechanical including, but not limited to photocopying, recording, scanning, digitizing, taping, web distribution, information networks or information storage and retrieval systems, except as permitted under Section 107 or 108 of the 1976 United States Copyright Act, without prior permission of the author. To obtain permissions to use content from this work, please submit written request to

ISBN- 13: 978-1-7323280-1-3

For further information, visit www.drmichaelmosley.com

Dedication

First, I thank my Heavenly Father, Jesus Christ and the power of the Holy Spirit for entrusting in me such an awesome gift that I will always cherish. In everything that I do, I pray that God always receives the glory! It is with extreme pleasure that I dedicate this book to those who have believed in my gift and ministry through the years and have supported me spiritually and financially.

To my mother, Ms. Patricia A. Mosley, whose love has carried me through many storms, my sister, Mrs. Pamela Drawsand, who called me and prophesied that God was depending on me to write.

I also thank my editorial friends, Ms. Heather Chimney, Ms. Sonia Person, and Ms. Kassilia Wright. You ladies made me sound good on paper.

To my church family, The Prophetic Institute for Prosperous Living and the many partners of MLM Ministries, for always hanging in there with me.

I also dedicate this book to my six manifested angels, my children, Benjamin, Christopher, Patrick, Jaden, Sir Michael and Mikayla! Thanks for being my biggest fans and always understanding when Daddy has to be on the road! I love you!

Last, but certainly not of least importance, I thank my personal cheerleader, who has been by my side routing me on to greater success, my darling wife, Annilia! I love you very much and thanks for EVERYTHING!

Preface

To be success minded means to have a mindset that supports progress. It means that one has the thoughts to bring about increase. One must keep in mind your thoughts create the environment in which we all live. You are living the way you are because of your thought process.

Understanding the Ministry of Prophecy can and will help you reach your achievable status of success! Prophecy comes as a means to keep your thoughts and energies focused on your desired Godly outcome.

Through Prophetic Ministry, I have gained much success. I've been guided into better decisions, better insights regarding personal situations and even correction towards choices that would not be in my best interest.

I have acquired a great deal of understanding about this profound ability, which I knew practically nothing about. As a child, I remember being afraid to go to sleep at night because I would see spirits in my room. Even in my adult life, I would hear voices and receive knowledge that I couldn't explain how I knew the information.

When I acknowledged my "calling" to minister, I had a vision of death. I didn't know who it was coming for, but I was assured it was headed towards my direction or to someone I knew. A few weeks later, I received the distressing call that my grandmother had just crossed over. I was devastated and shocked, because it was certainly unexpected.

This book that you hold in your hands is informative, inspirational, motivational, entertaining and short on purpose. I wanted to give a lot in a little bit of time. Time is very precious, and people are always rushing. They need encouraging and they often need it quickly.

You will find this unique concept shared throughout the book. It contains stories and thoughts that are designed to be short and effective, information that has the power to move you from one level to the next, if only you will open your mind and heart and allow that power.

Now relax and get ready to receive Successful Insight through Prophetic Revelations!

Table of Contents

Understanding Prophecy	7
Dimensions of Prophetic Ministry	16
The Prophetic Office	25
Prophets Are Not God's Replacements	40
The Power of the Prophet	51
Preparation to Receive Prophecy	60
Requirements for a Prophetic Manifestation	71
Financing God's Prophetic Voice	80
Beware of the False Prophet	93
"Why Hasn't My Word of Prophecy Come to Pass?"	110
Prophetic Communication	122
The Prophetic Ministry in Church	133
Testimonials	142

CHAPTER 1

UNDERSTANDING PROPHECY

"Do you hear anything for me?" asked the middle-aged lady sitting one seat over from me on the airplane. After the general questions "Where are you landing today?" and "Is this your first time in New York?" and, finally, "What type of work do you do?" I told her I was a prophet.

I don't normally tell people at first that I am also a pastor because they have a tendency to shy away, and I want to make sure I create an environment that I can share or if need be to speak a divine message to them. Therefore, I allow the usage of my gift to open doors for me, or, rather, I allow my gift to open the opportunity to express God's love to many people. Proverbs 18:16 declares, *"A man's gift maketh room for him, and bringeth him before great men."*

With a gentle smile, as she politely moved her dreadlocks behind her ears to hear, she waited with great anticipation for me to speak to her with a prophetic word. Right before I was about to speak, she asked a more detailed question for me to answer: "What is my purpose?" I looked at this dear lady and my right ear began to tingle with a word for her. I told her she was a "behind-the-scene" type of woman. She is gifted with the ability to motivate people into change and even cultivate and nurture that change. I went further to tell this lady, "You are gifted to teach, and teaching will always be a passion for you." "Give me a high five," she responded, as her hand shot up in the air.

As the plane began to descend into New York, my ears started to clog from the air pressure; however, I had to strain to hear how excited this lady was. She shared with me that everything I said to her was right on the money. She told me she was a teacher, a profession that she had recognized passion for ever since she was a little girl. Currently, she was teaching English at college in New York! It was so encouraging to her to know that she was fulfilling her purpose from God here on earth.

God Always Has Something to Say

I have come across many people who desire to know if God has anything to share with them. God always has something to share with His children. Well, what about the unbeliever or the non-Christian? Does God have something to say to them? You bet! God really desires to inform many that He is real and has an overwhelming love for everyone regardless of beliefs.

While living in a previous home in Spring, Texas, my air conditioning went out, and if anybody knows me, they know I cannot live without air conditioning. As a child I prayed to God to give me a job or career working inside with air conditioning! Anyway, a repairman came to fix the evaporator coil on the air conditioner. He was a foreigner, and just out of curiosity, I asked him what religion he was. This very nice man shared with me his religion and that he did not believe in Jesus as the Saviour. Well, I was not going to start a debate with this gentleman. In fact, I was a little tired because the air was out, and I wanted him to hurry up and fix the problem.

However, when he did fix the air conditioner and was preparing to leave, my right ear popped open. I could sense God wanting to deliver a word to this man. I was very apprehensive because I didn't want the man to feel I was pressuring him to convert to Christianity, which would, in turn, make him feel uncomfortable. I just wanted to be sure that he would feel the love of God.

Of course, I obeyed God and began to share a word with this man. "Excuse me," I said while we both stood in the foyer of my home, by this time the air was repaired, and I was standing right under the cooling vent. "I have a gift from God that allows me to see things about people's lives and to hear messages from God." I proceeded to tell the man about some family issues regarding his daughter, a health issue regarding his wife and some devastating financial problems he had been facing. I also shared with him some things God desired to do to enrich his difficult situations.

Afterwards, he looked at me in pure amazement. With a heavy accent and broken English, he asked, "You hear God just like I'm talking to you?" I told him, "Yes, and when the things I have said come to pass for your life, I ask you to do one thing: I want you to tell our loving Father, "Thank you!"

A few weeks later, I received a phone call. Upon answering the phone, I recognized it was the Arabian repairman. He had kept my number from the invoice. He shared with me that he went home and told his family of the things I said to him and how they were so amazed at the accuracy of the message. Yet, beyond that, he told me that some things were already starting to happen for him according to my predictions. And, with a calming and grateful tone, he stated to me that he told our Heavenly Father, "Thank you!"

Just as with my children, (I endeavor to constantly tell them how much I love them) God desires the same thing. God is always trying to get a message to people everywhere that He loves us so much that He sent His son, Jesus, to prove how much He loves us.

What God has to say may not be what we desire to always hear, yet He still has something to say. It's just like coming to your spouse today and saying, "I love you." Even though you said the same thing yesterday, it's still good to hear today. It's nothing new, but it's still refreshing and reassuring to hear.

Just When I Need Him Most

Prophecy comes to give us *"edification, exhortation, and comfort,"* according to 1 Corinthians 14:3. Through prophecy one is encouraged to know that God is aware of their current situation, whether good or bad. Not only is He aware, but He is concerned about our individual well-being. Knowing that God recognizes our frustrations and joys allows us to understand that we are never alone in whatever we may have or will face in our lives. God is not looking with a condemning eye to knock us across the head, but with a compassionate heart, waiting to express His love towards us.

There is a hymn written by William C. Poole that states, *"Just when I need Him, Jesus is near. Just when I falter, He's willing to cheer. He's willing to help you, willing to cheer, just when I need Him most!"* Prophecy is one-way God chooses to inform each of us that He is with us *"just when we need Him most!"*

What is Prophecy?

Prophecy is communicating the thoughts and will of God to mankind. Preaching and teaching the Word of God is a form of prophecy, which is known as foretelling. Yet, there is also another form of prophecy called forthtelling. Forthtelling is more of issuing predictions, which is the method of prophecy that I will expound upon in this book.

It must be understood that both forms of prophecy are needed for the prosperous growth of any individual. Predictive prophecy should create a desire for more understanding about God's love, which will direct our attention to those in teaching ministries. One person explained it beautifully to me like this: "Prophecy is like medicine; it helps to heal or increase health right now." However, in many cases the medicine must be accompanied with food. The understanding of God is the food needed in our lives, which enables the prophetic word to be activated.

God never just wants us to receive messages about new homes, cars, job situations, relationships, and, yet, we are not aware of the greatest prophecy. John 3:16

tells us of the greatest prophecy known to man: *"For God so loved the world that He gave His only begotten Son that whosoever believeth on Him should not perish but have everlasting life."* Outside of receiving prophetic insight about life's issues, if we follow the teachings us Jesus, He prophesied or predicted we will have everlasting life from earth to Heaven. What could be better?

Just think about it! If God speaks through the prophet and shares with you great truths, revelations, and promises about your earthly life, Heaven has got to be better. There's a lot God desires for us to achieve here on earth. He makes quite a few of those desires known through prophecy. He wants us to advance here on earth. However, there is going to come a time when God shall say to you and me, "Now, this next blessing for you, my child, is so big that the earth cannot contain it. Therefore, you are going to have to come home to Heaven and receive it." So, every blessing or accomplishment we make here on earth should serve as a motivator to follow and submit to God because it only gets better in Heaven!

It must also be understood that prophecy does not come as a substitute for your own personal spiritual relationship. However, it does come to make the Spiritual teachings more applicable to our current and familiar environments. In the Christian faith, we are taught with great conviction that the Bible is our source book. Everything we do should be based on the teachings of Jesus Christ held within our source book. Some people feel that since they received a word from God, in seminar or service, they don't need or neglect to study God's Spiritual principles. Remember, prophecy is only the mechanics. It must be accompanied with an understanding of faith which is the basic teachings given by the Holy Scriptures.

CHAPTER 2

DIMENSIONS OF PROPHETIC MINISTRY

By now, we understand that one of the ways God communicates His thoughts and desires to mankind is through prophecy. Then, there are people, like myself, who have been gifted by God with a special ability to speak for Him. These persons are equipped to hear with greater detail than normal from the counsel of God.

Persons chosen to be God's mouthpiece are called "prophets." God communicates to the prophet a divine message to be delivered, and the prophet simply relays that message. It is the job of the prophet to express the heart and thoughts of God and to express them plainly to the minds of individuals.

There are three dimensions of prophetic ministry: First, the spirit of prophecy: then, the gift of prophecy; and, finally, the prophetic office.

Spirit of Prophecy

I believe everyone has the ability to be utilized by the spirit of prophecy. This is when someone will be unctioned to release words of comfort to the hearers, mainly during a time of prayer or meditation. This person does not necessarily operate predominantly in prophetic ministry, but their spirit was open for God's message to be revealed to them.

Many times, the spirit of prophecy is also activated when one is in the midst of other prophets. A perfect example of this is found in 1 Samuel 10:5-10.

> *"After that thou shalt come to the hill of God, where is the garrison of the Philistines: and it shall come to pass, when thou art come thither to the city, that thou shalt meet a company of prophets coming down from the high place with a psaltery, and a tabret, and a pipe, and a harp, before them; and they shall prophesy:*
>
> *And the Spirit of the LORD will come upon thee, and thou shalt prophesy with them, and shalt be turned into another man.*

And let it be, when these signs are come unto thee, that thou do as occasion serve thee; for God is with thee.

And thou shalt go down before me to Gilgal; and, behold, I will come down unto thee, to offer burnt offerings, and to sacrifice sacrifices of peace offerings: seven days shalt thou tarry, till I come to thee, and shew thee what thou shalt do.

And it was so, that when he had turned his back to go from Samuel, God gave him another heart: and all those signs came to pass that day.

And when they came thither to the hill, behold, a company of prophets met him; and the Spirit of God came upon him, and he prophesied among them."

In this passage of Scripture, Samuel gives Saul prophetic instructions and predicts to him some things that are going to happen for him. One experience Samuel spoke of to Saul was that he was going to encounter some prophets while traveling, and, while in their company, that same spirit to prophesy will come upon him and he, too, shall prophesy.

This alerts us to a danger, as well as to a glorious opportunity for all to be used at some point in time by prophetic ministry. God enjoys using His children to convey the messages of His heart to others but be aware that He may not be using you to do this on a consistent basis as a prophet. However, appreciate the time or times God may choose to use you as His mouthpiece.

There are those persons who view the prophetic office as one of glamour and prestige. They desire to have that same advantage of seeing into the future for people and it appears to gain one more clout, or so it seems. I would encourage one to be mainly excited to be a child of God and cherish the moments of feeling His divine love.

Gift Of Prophecy

The gift of prophecy operates within a person for the general up-building, encouraging and comforting of the church and individuals. (1 Corinthians 12:10; 14:3,4) Those persons utilizing this gift have a tremendous ability to bring forth encouragement to people. This is their main purpose, which differs from the prophetic office.

The prophetic office goes into further areas that we will discuss later.

Have you ever met anyone whom when after you spoke with them, they made you feel you can do the impossible? It appears that every time you come in contact with this person, they are so full of positive energy. They are just a breath of fresh air. No matter what you are trying to accomplish, after communicating or listening to that person, you feel that you can do whatever you can dream!

I have had the pleasure of meeting several people like this. Sitting in my living room conversing with this older, precious lady, who maintained a very rich relationship with Jesus Christ, made me realize something. She would always share positive words of motivation towards me. In her eyes, there was nothing I could not do. While gleaning from her motivation, I told her that she had a gift of encouragement. It was then the Lord whispered in my right ear, "She has the gift of prophecy!"

Many people who serve as great motivators, whether it is pastors, teachers, parents or loved ones, have the gift of prophecy. Why is it that we feel so uplifted after attending a Les Brown, Tony Robbins, or an Iylana Vanzant meeting or any other motivational speaker? It is because they prophetically speak to us to achieve and live our dreams. For many years, millions of people, daily tuned in to the "Oprah Winfrey Show" to be inspired to achieve their best in life. It is because she maintains the gift of prophecy.

"You can do it!" This is the constant message of someone with the gift of prophecy. These people consistently predict to us that we can accomplish our desires. Directly or indirectly, these people carry the message of Jesus Christ in Matthew 19:26: *"With men this is impossible, but with God all things are possible."*

I have been privileged to have had, and still maintain, some people around me that will consistently utilize their gift of encouragement (prophecy) to motivate me.

If I'm trying to lose weight or start an exercise regimen, I need somebody with the gift of prophecy to help me. One morning, while out jogging, if that's what you want to call it, my trainer was on the side of me prophesying. She kept telling me that I could do it, and to keep moving, and don't stop, and that I had to get in shape for the great things God had in store for my life. The more my trainer prophesied, the more I kept going. However, I sho' was glad when that workout was over!

Persons with the gift of prophecy have an overall vision of what's ahead. They may not know the specifics of your goal, but they can generally see that it is possible. Then, again, they may not be able to see the idea you may have in full focus, yet, they believe in you or the powers of creativity that encircle your life, making any and everything possible.

Many years ago, when I first arrived in Las Vegas to do a meeting, I fell in love with the city. Many people, especially my religious colleagues, refer to Las Vegas as "Sin City." I refer to that beautiful city as the "City of Creativity!" As I was escorted through the city by a local pastor, Dr. Anne Jones, I viewed the beautiful hotels and soon realized that if one can think of it, it can be done. That is the mentality of the city! Wow! In the midst of all that desert land lays a great message of prophecy, being "It can be done!"

A dear friend invited me to dinner once, and she shared with me how, that summer she was taking some youth of her church to a summer camp. Immediately, I responded, "Sharon, that's a great idea; however, consider not just doing it for your church, but open it to other churches or organizations that are not large enough to do it themselves." I went on to say, "You may even be able to get donations from businesses for the travel expenses; and in addition to taking the children to visiting camps, go visit different cities and see other environments." In the midst of my excited blabbering, my friend stopped me and with a slight grin she told me, "Michael, somebody can tell you that they want a peanut butter and jelly sandwich and you will figure out a way and encourage them to open a restaurant!" Hey, what can I say? It's just my gift of prophecy working.

It becomes very vital for all of us to remain faithful in our various talents or gifts. Don't try to fulfill the role of the prophet if God did not give you that responsibility. There are many persons in the religious community labeling themselves as prophets for a sense of greater recognition, when they really are not prophets. Many pastors utilize the title "prophet" or "apostle", especially in African-American churches, in an attempt to attract parishioners who, desire prophetic ministry.

I've encountered several preachers who are excellent ministers, but they are not prophets. An occasional prophetic word does not garner someone the office of the prophet. Be that awesome teacher that will help clarify understanding in the word of God. If you desire advancement, pray and see if the advancement you are striving for is the will of God. All can't prophesy. Somebody is needed to sing, teach, usher, and even be the janitor for the church. Likewise, everybody can't be the bank president. Someone is needed to be the teller, secretary, beautician, nurse, etc. Each person will find success in life if he would just do what they are called to do. God has millions of ways to prosper you. Remember Deuteronomy 8: 18: *It is God who is the source of our wealth, not the job itself.*

CHAPTER 3

THE PROPHETIC OFFICE

The office of the prophet is an extension of the gift of prophecy operating in a higher realm of ministry. The office of the prophet goes beyond general encouragement and motivation into more specific areas. The prophet is gifted and authorized by God to flow in areas of guidance, instruction, rebuke, judgment, revelation, and whatever God chooses to speak for the edification of the hearers

The prophet has an ability to see or perceive a clearer, more detailed picture of what is to be shared with the listeners, as opposed to persons with the gift of prophecy who can only see the general overview. Many persons I've seen who claim the office of a prophet need and can receive more development into the office. I've seen so many of these dear people that only give what I call "generic prophecies."

Be Careful of Generics

I've heard many prophets say things like, "The Lord sees your storm and the storm is over." Well, who in most of our meetings doesn't have a "storm" he is going through? If you are a real prophet, tell me more about my "storm," which will assure me God does see me and that you are not a phony.

We are living in desperate times, and many people are looking for a true and authentic word from the Lord. After such events as September 11, School shootings, Hurricane Katrina, and so many other catastrophes, millions are asking and searching for spiritual answers. With that type of pressure from mankind, we, as prophets, can't afford to present our Lord as "generic."

It is important that those who feel they possess the calling into the prophetic office, to develop that calling. Later on, we will discuss how to develop your calling or gift. Out of several books on prophetic ministry, many fail to present clear methods in developing one's prophetic gift or office.

The prophetic ministry, within the prophetic office, has developed towards a more matured level, which is why God can reveal tremendous revelations to the prophet. He is not so easily moved or frightened by what is revealed to him. Therefore, God can trust him with specific details regarding someone's life.

The job of the prophet is to let others know the thoughts of God regarding their lives. As a prophet, I am to make you aware of God's presence and concern towards the situations you are facing. I am also to predict or foretell God's future plans for your life.

The prophet comes as a reminder from God that He has not forgotten you and He is aware of what you are going through physically and spiritually. This is why many people want to know if there is a word from the Lord, that they may be reassured that God knows about their situation. When battling with illnesses, trying to hold down a job, raising a family, or paying bills with not enough money, it will appear that God is not around. Oh, but, yes, He is right there!

After getting my haircut one day, back when I had hair, I was just about to walk out of the empty barber shop. The owner beckoned for me to wait and motioned for me to come back towards him. All of a sudden, this strong, middle-aged, muscular man, who just finished cutting my hair, began to cry and desperately asked for me to pray for him. As he held out his hand towards me, he stated, "Please, please, just pray for me and tell me whatever God tells you!"

I was shocked because I never told this gentleman that I was a prophet. Several times we would discuss the goodness of serving the Lord and being a Christian, but never did I tell him I was a prophet. I didn't know if he perhaps had seen me on television or heard me on the radio, which, right now, it didn't matter. Now was the time to share with this disturbed man a comforting word from God.

I prayed and shared some words of prophecy with him that I heard from God. Seeing the tears flow from his eyes made a tremendous impact on my life. I could sense he was going through many pressures and just needed to be reassured that God was still around. With those tears in his eyes, he was so grateful for the words in which I had spoken to him and he shared with me that everything was so accurate. As he wiped his eyes, I felt he was wiping away his worries and was now able to feel a sense of relief that God had not forgotten him. I remember his last words to me: "You just don't know how much I really needed that!"

Just like that barber, many of us crave a word from the Lord just to serve as a reminder that *"yea though I walk through the valley of the shadow of death, I will fear no evil, for thou are with me."* (Psalms 23:4) With this comforting prophecy, prediction, or promise comes a victorious thought that we are winners. Being that God knows about our struggles, He has prepared a way for us to be free from the struggle. Psalms 34:19 prophetically speaks or one can say that this scripture predicts: *"Many are the afflictions of the righteous: but the Lord delivers them out of them all."* Even I have experienced many of those afflictions.

Never Stop Prophesying

I tell everyone I meet that I do enjoy my job as being a prophet. However, there have been several times when I didn't want the job. I can distinctly remember colleagues of mine who would prophesy to me and they would tell me the strangest thing. More than one person has shared this word that God impressed them to tell me: "Never stop prophesying!" One person, Pastor J. R. Winston, went further to tell me that even if I had to prophesy to a glass of water to "never stop prophesying!"

At the time, I couldn't understand why God was issuing such a word to me. Knowing that prophecy has a futuristic dimension to it, I knew there had to be a future twist to such a word. And there was! As time proceeded in my life, I can honestly say there came a point in which I didn't want to prophesy anymore. I began to feel used and unappreciated by people, and even by God.

I had so many negative things happen in my life that I felt deserted by God. My pain was great. After spending hours reading every book I could get my hands on about prophetic ministry, praying, days fasting and honestly trying to walk in a strong level of integrity, it appeared nothing would go right for me. I faced bankruptcy, foreclosure, divorce, decrease in church ministry, and so much more!

I know these are not the things one really desires to talk about in ministry. However, I learned that through our struggles and pains God is so beautifully enhancing our gifts and callings. Through all of my challenges, and even being angry with God, my spirit became more sensitive to God's voice in prophesying about many of life's issues. This was all part of my makings of being a prophet.

Not that everyone must go through the same traumatic events, but we will go endure certain obstacles to help perfect our prophetic ministries. One purpose for such trials is to provide the prophet with a greater sense of humility. Yet, this is with any profession. Many trials or difficulties come to prove to you how strong you really are! God does not desire His prophets to speak in a way of arrogance or intimidation, but with love and humility. When we are able to remember and be honest about our feelings of everyday life, we, as prophets, can help others.

I can discern better now the feelings of a person contemplating suicide because I felt those same feelings. Once, after sharing my testimony of hardships, one person wrote me an e-mail and rebuked me for my feelings of suicide. They instructed me that a "real leader" of God should never feel the spirit of suicide or feel like giving up. I disagree, for through my experience, I am able to sense and detect that suicidal spirit upon others because I've been there.

At one point, I couldn't understand why a lot of men were apprehensive about getting married. However, through my marital difficulties, I then understood, as that was the way I felt after my divorce. Now, after encountering those feelings I'm able to prophesy to persons going through such situations with greater sensitivity, which increases my level of accuracy.

In whatever ability one may have from God, some trials are going to be experienced. The tests are not for our failing, but to serve as motivation and proof of Psalms 34:19 which states, *"Many are the afflictions of the righteous, but the Lord delivereth him out of them all."*

Relationship Is Better than Religion

Well, what about the times when I just messed up on my own? (And we have all done that at one time or another.) We find in these situations that it is not about us, but, rather, it is about Him. He created us and knows all about us, and there are times when we go through things only to discover that, without Him, the obstacle is too much to bear. Sure, we go to church and we quote the Lord's Prayer, but He is looking and searching for something deeper. He doesn't want us to be in religion with Him, but, rather, in a relationship with Him. There is a difference!

In religion, we are doing things for the sake of the religion that we are in. We are mainly following certain rules to appease the physical spiritual leaders governing the various religious bodies. For instance, the denomination or religion I grew up in taught you can't listen to any R&B, jazz, rap or even classical music. I remember as a little boy listening to music on the radio and if the song didn't say anything about Jesus in the first verse, I turned the radio dial. Ladies in my religion couldn't wear pants, make-up, and not even a skirt with an inch split in it! I'm serious!

When I was about seven or eight years old, my mother and sister would hate to take me shopping with them for clothes. As soon as my sister would pull out a skirt with a split, I would immediately rebuke her and remind her that Missionary So-and-So said that's "not holy." Back then, I was characterized by some of my peers as a "church nerd;" however, I kept everyone saved according to the religion!

However, in a relationship with our loving Father, He is not so concerned with the rules of religion. As time continues and more and more theologians have begun to so beautifully explain the written word of God, many have come to understand that one's clothes has very little to do with salvation. Salvation has everything to do with the heart and what it is that one believes. In a relationship with God, one is more concerned with loving God from our heart and exemplifying that love towards others.

Religion becomes very judgmental about appearance, whereas relationship is concerned with service to our fellow man. One of my favorite gospel artist alluded to this truth. While accepting a Stellar award, Yolanda Adams spoke with great authority to the religious body of people not to be concerned with what mainstream gospel artists have on, but to focus on the goal of helping others. She further alluded to the fact that one must first get the attention of people to be able to help them.

The pants, laced outfits, long nails, and leather

jackets have replaced the choir robes many gospel artists used to wear. Yet, in this prophetic change of attire, it has increased the listenership of gospel music. In fact, I look at a lot of our gospel artist today as musical prophets, who by their actions have prophesied that God loves us all. In addition to Yolanda Adams, thank God for Kirk Franklin, Mary Mary, Israel Houghton, and others who have musically performed one of the most powerful commandments in which Jesus gave. According to Luke 14:23, Jesus said, *"Compel them to come in, that my house may be filled."* The highway and hedges are prophetically speaking of outside the church.

Compel means to attract. We, as Christians, are to attract people to Christianity, not force them. And, certainly we are not to scare them towards or away from Christianity with lists of rules having nothing to do with salvation.

If you are going to be a sincere prophet of God, you can't be tied down with religion. There are several instances in the Bible when the prophet had to defy the religion of that time and do some interesting things. Take, for instance, the prophet Hosea, who was instructed by God to marry a prostitute. It symbolized God's love and forgiveness. (Hosea 1:1-11) Also, consider Isaiah who walked about naked for three years, demonstrating captivity for Egypt. (Isaiah 20:2-4) Now if someone in mainstream Christianity did these actions today, I believe they would be greatly ridiculed and dishonored.

The Saints Are Too Slow

Once, I was in the dressing room preparing to go on set to do a television taping. While looking into the mirror, my right ear popped open and I heard the Lord say, "The devil is ahead, and the saints are too slow!" I associate "devil" to equate the spirit of "fear!" Therefore, "fear is ahead, and the saints are too slow!" At first this statement puzzled me, and then I received the interpretation. For some time, God had been instructing me to do something that I felt I would be blasted for by the religious community! Let me backtrack a little.

Years ago, while I was watching television, the infamous Miss Cleo would come on with her commercial for her psychic hotline. Every time I would see that commercial, I would cringe. After doing this for so many times, I guess God got tired of me and corrected me with a tremendous reprimand. I sensed the Lord telling me one afternoon after viewing her commercial, "Why are you cringing or getting upset with her? She's just doing her job." He went on further to say, "You are just jealous that she's doing what you can do, but you are not. There are many people looking for an answer to their problems; and they don't know you exist, so people call who they see." Of course, we now know that "Miss Cleo" was an actress, but God was trying to elevate my prophetic responsibility.

At that point, God informed me to do something about it. I would always say in my church meetings that whatever the "psychics" are gifted to do, I could do also. Well, God told me that day to prove it. He instructed me to start a "prophetic phone line," where people could call me to hear a word from God regarding their concerns. Needless to say, I refused because I knew the religious community would blackball me. This was my thinking due to the forces of religion and not in response to a trusting relationship with God.

Well, while looking in the mirror that day, waiting to go on the television set, God encouraged my heart again to obey Him. He showed me how the forces of evil had spread so quickly in drugs, suicide, and depression.

And now we must ignore the judgment of the religious community in order to focus and reach the hurting community, by any means necessary.

I finally obeyed the voice of God, and the gates of hell broke loose within the religious community in my city of Houston. I advertised on a gospel station, and the station became flooded with calls to cancel my commercial. Many preachers vanished from my acquaintance and openly spoke against me in their pulpits. I was labeled as one you had to "pay to pray" or the "prophet for profit." These sayings really did hurt me. Yet, and still, whenever my prophetic line would ring and someone informed me how they were greatly helped, it made all the drama worth it.

Now, we have replaced the hotline with online prophetic ministry. People today are still meeting with me online, asking important questions and receiving answers through the prophet from God! Yet, believe it or not, some 20 years later there are still some preachers trying to discredit me for having a phone line for people to call for prayer and mainly that there was a fee attached to the phone call. Yet, these same preachers ask for an offering, sometimes two or three offerings, from the parishioners in the pews weekly! What's the difference?

I encourage you, whether you are a prophet of not, to always obey the voice of God. I proudly join the ranks of others who are using their gifts and talents from God to help people at any cost. No, it is not always popular; but, if it's God, it is always productive!

God is not calling everyone to do the same thing. God needs someone to do something different to prove the scripture *"I will do a new thing,"* according to Isaiah 43:19. Everyone doing the same thing, prophesying to the same people in the same manner, becomes boring and unproductive. God needs someone He can use to help get the attention of mankind in a new and exciting way. Therefore, in order to be one of God's prophets with a new daring assignment from God, one must be in a relationship with God as opposed to a religion.

CHAPTER 4

PROPHETS ARE NOT GOD'S REPLACEMENTS

God always desires for us, as His children, to have a relationship with Him. He wants us to be able to come and talk with Him about anything. Whatever is troubling your mind, God has issued us an open invitation to feel free to discuss our issues with Him. Jesus says in Matthew 11:28, *"Come unto me, all ye that labour and are heavy laden, and I will give you rest."*

The prophet or any ministerial leader is not here on earth to replace the presence of God in one's life. There are some people who feel as if they don't necessarily need to pray because they can just go to the prophet and hear a message from God. Then there are others who feel that the prophet has all the answers to their problems, which is just not so!

In many of my meetings, I do offer a chance for people to ask me questions about their life's issues. To the best of my ability, I give them the answer I sense from God. However, there have been times when I couldn't release some answers or just part of the answer because God desired to talk with that person on an individual basis. There are many things God desire to reveal to His children in prayer and meditation.

Look at it this way. Although you may have a babysitter to watch and care for your children, you, as the parent, wouldn't want the child to stop communicating with you. You still desire for the child to come and talk with you about their problems and joys. The babysitter is not to take the role of the parent, but to maintain the order or care of the parent towards the child. Likewise, the prophet is not to be looked upon as a substitute for a relationship with God. Remember, everyone has an ability to hear from God and He desires to talk with you, just as He communicates with the prophet. The prophet's ability to hear may be a little more intense than on average, but each believer can have communication with God.

One of the first commandments in the Bible is

"Thou shall have no other God before me." (Exodus 20:3) This includes the office of the prophet. We are God's representative, not His replacement. There is absolutely nothing that can replace a genuine relationship with our loving Father.

I am very grateful to know the secretary of a prestigious business leader; however, it sure would be even better to know the leader. Well, someone would say, "Why should I even bother with listening to the secretary when I know the leader?" It's because there are some special favors the leader has entrusted into the hands of his secretary which are to be given only to me. As prophets, we are trusted by the Lord to issue those things which he has specially designated for you because of your relationship with Him. I'm quite sure you wouldn't mind if your friend or business partner left the check for your requested amount with the secretary or the janitor, just as long as you get it! The one thing that is important to realize is that it is because of your relationship that you know your friend will not let you down. This reminds me of the singer Fantasia Barrino, was to appear for another audition for "American Idol" but she got there a bit late. It was the janitor who took the risk to open the door and allowed her to enter the next audition. Of course, we all know, she won the official title that year of "American Idol."

It is true that many prophets and spiritual leaders have some outstanding gifts and abilities from God. Some are gifted with areas of healing, causing blind eyes to open, paralyzed limbs to become mobile, yet others may dictate to you the deepest thoughts or ideas of your heart, yet, we are still not the Supreme God.

After bringing forth healing to a crippled man in Lystra, the natives of the land began to perceive Paul and Barnabas as gods, being in the same category with Jehovah. Paul instructed the people that they were men as they were and for them to turn their hearts and beliefs towards the living God (Acts 14:818). It is wonderful to have great respect for spiritual leaders, but never put them in the same category as the God of the universe. Remember, that before there was the prophet, there was the man. It is that part of the man which may not always live up to your expectations: but God, the true source of fulfillment, will never let you down.

God, The Prophet

In fact, the first character of God seen in scripture is that of the prophet.

"In the beginning God created the heaven and the earth.

And the earth was without form, and void; and darkness was upon the face of the deep. And the Spirit of God moved upon the face of the waters.

And God said, Let there be light: and there was light."

Genesis 1:1-3

God said, "Let there Be!" He spoke into existence what was to be done to meet His needs and His desires. God wanted to be sure that you and I had this same ability. However, God also chose to embody such an ability in a greater dimension in people we call "prophets."

Psalms 82:6 describes us as "gods": "*I have said, Ye are gods; and all of you are children of the most High."* We are not on the same level with Jehovah God; however, we are extensions of God, just as our children are replicas or extensions of us. This is another reason why we were created in His image, that we can do the things He does.

Many people describe the prophet as one who foretells (proclaims or preaches the word of God), but, mainly, they are described as one who FORTHTELLS (one who predicts the futuristic will of God). Now, it must be understood that the prophet is one who speaks as God's mouthpiece. He speaks as a direct communicator from God. The Prophet carries the voice (judgment, verdict) of God, as was the case with Hezekiah and the prophet Isaiah (2 Kings 20:1-7).

It must also be known and realized that the prophet also carries a special power or authority from God. This power has been demonstrated several times in the Bible through the prophet Elijah.

- 1 Kings 17   Elijah increased the food supply of the woman at Zarapath.
- 1 Kings 18:41 Elijah asked and received rain.
- 2 Kings 1 Elijah called for fire to burn Ahaziah's messengers.

Even the first recorded miracle of Jesus demonstrated His office of being a prophet. In St. John 2 when Jesus turned water into wine, He wasn't utilizing the Pastoral office, the Evangelist office, the Teacher office, nor the Apostolic office. It was the Prophetic. This is so because Jesus called in, through a non-verbal method, what He needed and/or desired.

In the first actions of God and His son, Jesus, we don't see them forthtelling of an event, as in the many definitions of a prophet. However, what they do is bring about a current action that will meet the need or desire NOW! The prophet has the ability to meet your need NOW!

God spoke to me and told me, "You not only predict, but you mainly dictate!" Yes, it is true: prophets have the power to dictate to your circumstances a change and cause it to be so. Just look at the actions in the previous examples of Elijah. In Biblical times, whenever there was a need for success, wealth and prosperity, even the kings would call on the prophets. (2 Kings 8:8) Even today, whenever there is a need for increase in one's life, there's a need for the prophet; but, also, a need for your belief in God.

"Believe in the LORD your God, so shall ye be established; believe his prophets, so shall ye prosper." 2 Chronicles 20:20b

We must understand the Prophetic office is a direct dimension of Jesus' anointing. It was through His prophetic power that He spoke on the ship and stopped the wind from beating against the boat. It amazed the disciples and they stated, *"What kind of man is this?"* Why? Because He dictated to the universe what He wanted to happen.

"Now it came to pass on a certain day, that he went into a ship with his disciples: and he said unto them, Let us go over unto the other side of the lake. And they launched forth.

But as they sailed he fell asleep: and there came down a storm of wind on the lake; and they were filled with water, and were in jeopardy.

And they came to him, and awoke him, saying, Master, master, we perish. Then he arose, and rebuked the wind and the raging of the water: and they ceased, and there was a calm.

And he said unto them, Where is your faith? And they being afraid wondered, saying one to another, What manner of man is this! for he commandeth even the winds and water, and they obey him."

Luke 8:22-25

The Impossible Prophesied

Once during a time of meditation, God told me, "Michael, as My prophet, the impossible lies within you!" He then led me to read Matthew 19:26, where in Jesus said, *"With man this is impossible, but with God all things are possible."* As the day went by and I was trying to understand what God was saying, I kept hearing God say in my right ear, "Impossible." Later, I realized He was trying to get me to divide the word into "I'M POSSIBLE." I soon realized wherever it seems impossible, just remember "I'M POSSIBLE."

In understanding that principle, God gave me a new interpretation of that same scripture. I'm going to take this scripture out of context just a little in order to reveal the message God spoke to me. Instead of understanding it to say, "With man this is impossible, but with God all things are possible." God informed me that as the people began to prosper, it must be understood as "WITH MAN, THIS IS I'M POSSIBLE BECAUSE WITH GOD ALL THINGS ARE POSSIBLE!"

In other words, standing with Mrs. Jones is God, a.k.a. "I'm Possible." God is with her to prove that with His power coupled with her desires, anything is possible! Therefore, each of us must remember the "I'm Possible" is with us. This is why some people can understand the virgin birth of Jesus. It's because the "I'm Possible" was with Mary, making anything possible. Yet, it must be realized that even with the birth of Jesus, the "I'm Possible" action of Jesus' birth started with a prophecy.

> *"And the angel said unto her, Fear not, Mary: for thou hast found favour with God.*
>
> *And, behold, thou shalt conceive in thy womb, and bring forth a son, and shalt call his name JESUS."*
>
> *Luke 1:30, 31*

Now, certainly, that's the work of the "I'm Possible." Even now, when prophecy is spoken in our lives, we must be open to believe that it is possible because God is always possible.

I was surprised once when a lady came to me and showed me her new vehicle. She had bought a brand-new luxury SUV. She told me I had prophesied the exact make and model of the car and that it would be brand new, not pre-owned. She went on to tell me that she didn't really have faith for the vehicle, however, she went to look for it based on the prophetic word I gave her. She was convinced that I believed very strongly in what I stated to her. She told me, "Dr. Mosley, I went off of your faith in the 'I'm Possible.'" To her amazement, she was approved for the car and now she doesn't need my faith anymore. She is now open to the power of the "I'm Possible" for herself.

CHAPTER 5

THE POWER OF THE PROPHET

It has been stated that prophets can't do anything without first hearing from God. This is not necessarily true. God has given the prophet authority to do several things without having to hear from Him. It's just like working in law enforcement. The police just can't come and enter your property when they desire; they must have a search warrant. However, when they get the search warrant, they have the authorization to enter when they deem so. If a police officer suspects one is driving under the influence of a drug, he has the right to stop your vehicle and investigate the matter without calling in for permission.

So, it is with a prophet. God has given the prophet the ability to speak many things without hearing the direct instructions from God. Just like a police officer can give you a warning or a citation, so can the prophet bring forth change in your life at their discretion.

The Prophet Said It!

Some things will not happen for you until the prophet speaks, according to 1 Kings 17:1. God told Elijah rain would not enter the land until the prophet spoke for it to be so. Therefore, it is true that everyone needs the special gift of the prophet. Many theologians will say whatever God has for His people, they shall receive it thereby, claiming that there is no need for the prophetic voice.

Well, let's examine this concept in our present-day society, using our judicial system. If you have been unjustly treated and entitled to financial compensation for your pain and suffering, one would believe it is God's will for you to receive your compensation.

Understanding that God establishes and respects order, you are going to need the consent of a judge in order for you to receive your entitlement. Therefore, beyond any doubt you need God's power to bring about His will; but you also need the judge, who is responsible to be receptive and to issue orders that will carry out the will of God.

There are many gifts God desires to give to mankind; however, he established order regarding some things. Yes, there are many things God will give individuals without the prophet speaking them into existence. Yet, there are some blessings that God does desire the prophet to pronounce over individuals as was done with Hezekiah.

> *"In those days was Hezekiah sick unto death. And Isaiah the prophet the son of Amoz came unto him, and said unto him, Thus saith the LORD, Set thine house in order: for thou shalt die, and not live.*
>
> *Then Hezekiah turned his face toward the wall, and prayed unto the LORD, And said, Remember now, O LORD, I beseech thee, how I have walked before thee in truth and with a perfect heart, and*

have done that which is good in thy sight. And Hezekiah wept sore.

Then came the word of the LORD to Isaiah, saying, Go, and say to Hezekiah, Thus saith the LORD, the God of David thy father, I have heard thy prayer, I have seen thy tears: behold, I will add unto thy days fifteen years.

Isaiah 38:1-5

God could have spoken to Hezekiah by other means; however, he chose to send the prophet Isaiah back to the home of Hezekiah. Upon the prophet's return, he was to speak of God's decision to add fifteen more years to the life of the king.

The Prophet as God's Representative

Many times, the prophet is to speak what God has decided regarding various situations. However, as I stated before there are many times when the prophet makes the decision on the behalf of God. As we discussed earlier, God has given the prophet certain authority as his representative. As a representative, one is to speak on the behalf of the sender. The representative has the power to make decisions, make statements, and even ask questions in proxy of the sender. However, it is imperative for the representative to have a solid understanding of the sender's desires in order to speak on their behalf.

This is the same with God and the prophets. As prophets, we must spend quality time with God in order to best represent Him. Yes, we have power to make decisions and to bless people; however, we must have a close relationship with God in order to do that. Yet, it must be understood the prophet does have the power to bless you and bring forth miracles into your life.

Take, for instance, the story in 2 Kings 4:8-17. Elisha prophesied to the Shunamite woman that she would have a child. Yet, before he prophesied the child, because the lady had been so nice to him, he asked her what she wanted him to do for her.

It is already understood that the prophet is not to replace God but is God's representative. Therefore, it is amazing to know that in order for the prophet to be God's representative, God has given the prophet power to act in His stead. This is why we see here in the scripture, Elisha, as a prophet, has been given an awesome power from God to grant the lady her heart's desire. Elisha did not have to consult God because he had already been given power to act in God's stead. It's also amazing to know that Elisha had been given power to grant her whatever it was that the precious lady desired.

I encourage you not to take the presence of a prophet lightly because in the mouth of that prophet could be a beautiful life changing experience for you.

It is also interesting to understand that the conception of that child for the Shunamite woman did not take place until the prophet spoke it. My very first prophecy I ever gave was to my sister. My sister and her husband had been trying to conceive a child without any results. One day, while I was in prayer, I prophesied to her and told her, "Pamela, in one year, you shall be with a child." Needless to say, after I said that to her, I became very nervous because I did not want to disappoint my sister, knowing how badly she wanted a child.

The doctors said it was impossible and then tried to give her other alternatives which may produce a pregnancy. My sister kept coming to me asking me about the alternatives throughout the course of that year, and each time I would hear God encourage me to trust my word that I gave her, and He would honor it. I didn't want that prophetic word to fail in fear of letting God and my family down.

It just so happened, the day I was going to pay a visit to my mother, my sister just so happened to be there, too. When I walked in the door, there were big smiles. My sister informed me that she had recently left the doctor's office. She told me to get ready for my nephew, for he was on the way! God did it! He honored the words of His prophet. By the way, my sister didn't give me a nephew then; but, rather, she gave birth to my beautiful little niece, Shaquilla, and then gave me two handsome nephews, Dominic and Stefan. Not bad, seeing that the doctors said it was impossible. But the prophet has power to announce and bring forth change! Please let it be noted the Prophet does have power to bring forth change in your life!

The Prophet's Curse

We must recognize the prophet also has power to curse the works of evil. 2 Kings 2:23-24 depicts a tragic story illustrating the prophet's ability to curse.

"And he went up from thence unto Bethel: and as he was going up by the way, there came forth little children out of the city, and mocked him, and said unto him, Go up, thou bald head; go up, thou bald head. And he turned back, and looked on them, and cursed them in the name of the LORD. And there came forth two she bears out of the wood, and tare forty and two children of them."

Once again, realize God has given the prophet power to speak words of blessings, as well as curses, into an individual's life. Yet, the prophet is not permitted to just go cursing individuals at free will. The prophet must possess the heart of God through constant fellowship with God to represent Him effectively.

This is also why a prophet must be very careful what they say, even casually, to individuals. A dear friend and I were laughing on the phone about how she didn't want to go to work. I told her, casually and not being serious, she better go because there was a raise waiting on her. To her and my amazement, she called me the next day and told me when she got to work, she had received an unexpected raise! Wow! I felt God had begun to caution me about being careful in everything that I say because of the power He has entrusted into my care.

Yes, there are many people who have experienced a prophetic curse, even in my ministry. It's not my desire to illustrate these examples of curses in my ministry due to my belief of God using curses as a method of correction, not a lifetime penalty that glorifies the prophet. It becomes surprising to me how I've heard other people professing to be in prophetic ministry, actually brag about people losing their jobs, homes and even their lives because of a prophetic curse. A curse never merits boastful statements to prove one's prophetic calling. It is only to serve as a reminder of the seriousness and great love and respect we should always maintain towards God and His messengers!

CHAPTER 6

PREPARATION TO RECEIVE PROPHECY

"I must tell you I didn't believe in any of this. I didn't believe anyone could predict the future or tell me about the issues of my life without knowing me. Yet, I must say after meeting you today, I am a believer!" These were the words of a young Jewish lady as she and her father approached me for a prophetic consultation in one of my seminars.

This dear lady, named Lauren, informed me how she came to me with an open heart to hear what was going to be revealed to her and her dad. She had heard great things about me and wanted to experience the gift I have firsthand. She was really here to support her father, who wanted to see me and make sure everything was really real. However, it was Lauren who really was greatly enlightened about the power of God through prophecy. In fact, about two weeks later, it was Lauren who called me to schedule a private prophetic counseling session with her entire family.

I thanked Lauren for her opened heart to experience God's prophetic power in me. I informed her everyone should approach a prophet with the same manner of openness. There are times in life when you come across people who are not open to anything. They don't even want to believe the weatherman. Older folk use to say that some just don't believe that "fat meat is greasy." Friends, you will have to open yourselves to experience a supernatural level from God.

Open Your Heart

One thing we must do in preparing ourselves to receive a prophetic word is to open up our hearts, meaning our mindset or way of thinking. Remember, no one knows everything; there is always something to be learned, to be gained, to be understood in this life. We don't always understand how the weatherman is able to predict the weather; so, instead, we develop a certain amount of faith in the weather predictions, which allows us to believe and act according to the predictions.

The same is with prophecy. We may not understand it completely, but we do understand that God is a mystery all by Himself. Prophecy has been done many times in the scripture in times past, and I say that it can still be done today.

According to Ephesians 4:11-14,

> *"And he gave some, apostles; and some,*
>
> *prophets; and some, evangelists; and some,*
>
> *pastors and teachers;*
>
> *For the perfecting of the saints, for the work of*
>
> *the ministry, for the edifying of the body of Christ:*
>
> *Till we all come in the unity of the faith, and of the*
>
> *knowledge of the Son of God, unto a perfect man,*
>
> *unto the measure of the stature of the fulness of*
>
> *Christ:*
>
> *That we henceforth be no more children, tossed to*
>
> *and fro, and carried about with every wind of*

doctrine, by the sleight of men, and cunning craftiness, whereby they lie in wait to deceive."

We have to understand why prophets are here. There are certain myths that we will have to get rid of in order that we may receive the gift of a prophet. Bear in mind, if we do away with prophecy, we will also have to do away with pastors, preachers and evangelists. Truth be told, we cannot discard any of them. Let's get rid of the myth so that we can really receive a word from God.

How long is prophecy supposed to be here? I am glad you asked that question? According to the scripture, until we all become one. According to my understanding, we are not all thinking the same thing. Churches are fighting churches; people are fighting people; and neighbors are fighting neighbors. We are in a terrible fix. Therefore, there will always be a need for pastors, teachers, apostles, prophets, and evangelists. This is what is known in the Christian community as the five-fold ministry.

As you can tell, prophets are yet needed. The next time you approach one, ask what it is that God wants to tell you, how you can help your fellow brother, and how you can better help yourself.

I'll admit, in this line of prophetic work, people will often challenge me. For instance, someone may say, "If you claim to be a prophet, then tell me what I ate for dinner last night." And in my mind, I am thinking, why should I tell you what you ate for dinner when you already know?

Prophecy is real. In order to fully understand it, you must first be open. You must have an established faith in God, a strong constitution that nothing can move you. I mentioned earlier that prophets do not replace God; yet, they are a source, a source that knows about you, what you are sometimes going through, and the circumstances that circumvent your life.

Believe in Prophecy

Secondly, you must have faith in prophecy, understanding that God is capable of speaking to you. Often God is yet speaking, revealing things from His heart to ours. God wants to let you know that He is real and that He loves you.

This is one reason, as I have stated many times,

that I hate generic prophecy. I train and encourage prophets to develop their ability to be as accurate as possible. It becomes comforting to the hearer that God does know about their issue and you, as God's messenger, are not simply guessing.

We will discuss in Chapter 9 how there are people in the world who are not real. They are not genuine; they are fake; they are a fraud. But God is not like that. He is real.

I remember once meeting a man that everyone referred to as Dr. Parker. Later, I found out he really wasn't a doctor at all. I told myself, you've got to be kidding. This man didn't even have a doctorate degree, but what made it worse: he proclaimed to be a dentist!

Just like Dr. Parker, some people are fake; and in order to know the difference, you have to check them out. There are some real genuine preachers; and, unfortunately, there are some fake ones. There are some people who genuinely love you beyond measure, and there are others who couldn't care less as to your well-being. You have to check them out to know who is real and who is not.

If by chance you are planning to attend a prophetic seminar, or what we call in the church, a prophetic revival, or a prophetic worship service, it would be good to say to yourself, "I am going to open myself up to God, meaning to have an open mind and I will have faith in the prophet and what I will hear."

Make Sure You Pray

Another thing I encourage everyone to do when they are going to receive a prophetic word or going to encounter the ministry of the prophet is to develop personal time with God before and after the encounter. I cannot say this enough: a prophet is not a replacement for God, he is only an instrument being used by God. With everything, even in prophecy, you will have to have a basis, an understanding of God and who He is.

How do we get that foundational knowledge of God? We acquire it through studying His word, by spending time with Him. We get it through praying and communicating with God, not just reading the scripture, but spending time with God and talking to him. Through studying, praying, fasting and developing that personal time with God, it will give you a spirit of discernment to determine whether or not the prophet's words are in agreement with what's in your spirit.

I remember once I prophesied to a young lady many years ago and it was a word she did not care to hear. It was a word from God stating there were some extra things she needed to do in order to better her life. I could immediately tell by her expression that she did not like what was spoken. I told her at that moment that if she did not receive the word, then go and fast for three days from 6:00 a.m.-12:00 noon and inquire of the Lord herself for the correction. Lastly, I asked her to inform me as to whether or not I was right or wrong.

She obeyed and fasted for the correct word and later stated to me, "Everything you told me was true and God revealed it to me. You were very much accurate, and, because of that, I repent for having such a doubtful spirit." It was also a relief to me because I never want to steer anybody wrong. She went on to state that she knew I was correct all along, but she just didn't want to believe it.

So often, we must maintain a foundational basis, a foundational knowledge about God. There are many

Christians that talk about what they believe, but a lot of them have not done their research in the scripture. Also, many of us believe certain things because it was taught to us, then that makes it true and scriptural. Deacon Jones said it, so it must be true. Rev. Jackson said it, and so it must be right. Well, we all have room for error, which is partly why there are so many different religions and denominations today.

Misinterpretation of the scripture started it all. However, each one of us are required to study scripture for ourselves as it states in 2 Timothy 2:15 *"Study to shew thyself approved unto God, a workman that needeth not to be ashamed, rightly dividing the word of truth."* No matter what religion is out there, everybody brings something of value to the table. No one person has the whole piece of pie.

While I'm there, I might as well let you know something else: There is no prophet who is 100% accurate. I know we desire to be. However, as long as we are humans, we can and will be in error many times. In fact, I will tell clients and parishioners if they don't agree with my prophetic statements, follow what they believe.

I remember I had a prophet to speak to me regarding a situation I was going through. I didn't agree with his statement. In fact, if I would have followed his direction, I would have lost everything in regard to my family. I don't believe the prophet intentionally desired to steer me wrong, but what he stated to me was just not accurate.

Have I made errors in my prophetic office? You better know it! However, none have been intentional. I remember when I first started prophesying, and I told this woman, she would be moving soon because I saw a lot of boxes packed in a house. Well, after the meeting, the lady came to me and told me she had just moved and was not looking to move again. The boxes I prophetically saw were the boxes in her living room waiting to be UNPACKED! I was extremely grateful this lady was very patient with my gift. I simply just had my signals mixed up.

However, there was another time when I told another woman she was going to purchase a new car. She politely told me she hadn't planned on it, since she just got a new car. Now, this time, I was sure in what I was seeing. The car she had was not the car I saw prophetically.

A few weeks later, the lady contacted me again. She was very amazed and excited to inform me the car she was driving was totaled-out in an accident. She wasn't hurt, but she did have to get another new car. It goes back to being open to receive. You may not totally understand it all, yet, you must allow your faith to push you to the next level.

Now, you may say, Michael, in the earlier chapters, you spoke to some who did not have to go through all of this, you simply spoke a word to them, you prophesied to them. So, are these steps really necessary to receive a prophecy? The answer is "no", they are not all necessary, but they help to make the process easier for the recipient of the word. It helps you to perceive the word better.

Chapter 7

Requirements for a Prophetic Manifestation

I have traveled to various places around the world, and one question remains the same: "Why hasn't this prophecy come to past?"

The hard-core truth is that many things are not just going to happen without your personal effort. The Bible states, *"Faith without works is dead"* (James 2:26); and I've met scores of people who have faith but have no works to follow. For some reason, we want God to do all the work. I've heard a slogan, "Nothing in life is free," and I partly believe it. Oh, sure, we say that salvation is free; but is it? Someone had to pay the price. So, in some way, it did cost.

If a prophet tells you that you will get a new car

soon, there still will be work involved. It may mean that you will have to use your energy to drive to the car lot to make a selection on the make, model and color. But before this, you may have to consult with the finance department to discuss what will be the down-payment and monthly notes. And before this, it may mean clearing and getting your credit repaired. In each instance, before receiving the gift, it took work on your part.

I remember once trying to purchase a new home. I was so excited. But before they would give me the home, I had to secure proper documentations of appraisals, employment verifications and credit reports. In addition, I had to verify certain items were paid on my credit report. Thank goodness I was blessed with the home, but it took work.

I was at a conference once, and a lady approached me asking me to tell her about her future husband. She came back about a month later stating, "Where is he?" Well, I never told her he was coming right away; and, besides, there were tons of things that she needed to do in preparation for him.

By the time she came to me the third month, she had really begun to wreck my nerves. It was obvious that she was looking for a Prince Charming, but in all honestly, she was not prepared to meet him. In her conversations with me, she appeared needy, desperate, an emotional basket-case and her self-esteem was below zero. I thought to myself, poor thing, what good would she be to any man in that condition? It was almost frightening.

Ask yourself as I do daily:

- Are you ready for a miracle?
- Have you prepared yourself mentally?
- Are you prepared for God's blessing and manifestation?
- Have you thrown out the old baggage?
- Have you cleaned up the debt?

I had to just come right out and tell the young lady, "Please don't wait for him to come along and pay all your bills. Do what you can yourself." Sorry to say, she got very upset.

If it is a new job you want, then fix up your resume. Enroll in a college or a vocational training school if that will help. Remember that faith without works is dead.

I remember another incident I had which was quite similar. I was speaking on the radio to a female caller who was single and asking about a relationship. I began telling her she keeps missing male attention because of her public presentation. I could see that she wore unattractive clothing and didn't give her hair the attention it deserves. Well, the caller was offended, but later that day she emailed me and told me how I was very accurate in her reading. That morning, she told me she changed her outfit, combed her hair differently and three hours later two men had approached her for a date!

The Bible gives a wonderful example in Luke 17: 11-14.

> *"And it came to pass, as he went to Jerusalem, that he passed through the midst of Samaria and Galilee.*
>
> *And as he entered into a certain village, there met him ten men that were lepers, which stood*

afar off:

And they lifted up their voices, and said, Jesus, Master, have mercy on us.

And when he saw them, he said unto them, Go shew yourselves unto the priests. And it came to pass, that, as they went, they were cleansed."

There were ten lepers and they wanted to be healed. As the first one started walking towards the direction of the priest, he still had leprosy. However, as they continued to walk, according to the directive of Jesus, the healing began. In all honesty, in order to see results, you've got to move in the direction of the prophecy.

One Sunday, I told this gentleman of my church who was looking for a job to get up early the next morning and look for a job. Prophetically, I knew there was a job waiting for him. However, my instructions to him was that he had to be up by 8a.m. and he would find just what he was looking for. Not everyone knows where

I live, but this man did because he did some work on my home before. To my surprise, that Monday night, I was up late in prayer and meditation when I noticed from my living room window that this gentleman was approaching my door. This man came to my home with a trunk-load of groceries as a token of thanks. He followed my directions and found the job that day that he had been looking for. I guess through all of his excitement, he didn't realize what time it was!

Prophecy comes along to put your mind on what God's mind is on. If you are planning a trip to California, why would you map out the directions to Hawaii? God is the compass; and, if you want to be one with him, you are going to have to map out a course that will lead you to Him.

Here are a few steps that I recommend:

- Write down what the prophet has revealed.
- Begin affirming your personal word. Make it an affirmation.

Affirm It!

Therefore, if a prophet says you are enstore for a

job change in sales making more money within four months, write the prophetic word down and turn it into an affirmation. Maybe something like, "I am gainfully employed and earning more money in sales." Repeat this affirmation to yourself every day. As you say it, you will begin to see your prophetic word began to manifest.

The same principle applies even when a word has been given of warning or avoidance. There have been times I've had to tell people about deaths or illnesses. In such cases, I encourage them to take preventive measures to cancel the word. However, if the person chooses to continue their life in the pattern that it's going, the word of warning is what I see manifesting.

I remember being in Minneapolis, Minnesota and I gave a prophetic word of warning to this young lady. I told her I saw her getting a cold or the flu and even told her an over-the-counter medication to get to avoid the illness. The next day, this lady came to my morning seminar and, with a little hostility, she spoke how she rebuked my word about the sickness due to the fact she had never been sick.

However, I proceeded to inform this lady to

remember how I also gave her a method to avoid the sickness. I went even further to tease the lady and tell her, "I don't know you, why would I want you to be sick?" She finally calmed down and laughed, but it appeared that she only focused on the part of the prophecy about her getting sick and it was only like a cold. Yet, she didn't seem to focus on the preventive measure which was also given in the prophecy. By the way, the lady still ignored my warning and a few days later, she caught a real nasty cold!

Even in cases like this, write an affirmation of prevention. It could be something like this, "I am living a healthy life with good eating habits." Now of course, this affirmation must be accompanied with proper actions to ensure effectiveness! Remember that your mind is the magnet that attracts the blessing of God towards you. Proverbs 23:7, paraphrased, emphasizes that whatever you think about the most is what you attract.

Many of you will get prophetic words about finance and prosperity. Make no mistake about it; you can have a financial breakthrough. It is possible, but you must take the necessary steps toward achieving through that prophecy.

- If it is about relationships and/or marriage, then prepare yourself.

- Prepare yourself mentally for a greater purpose to come into your life.

Whatever it is you desire, I am a living witness that it can happen in your life. Just be sure to go in the direction of the prophecy.

CHAPTER 8

FINANCING GOD'S PROPHETIC VOICE

This is a subject that a lot of prophets do not like to talk about. There are certain people who just do not like discussing money. We must first understand that money is no more than energy. Money is an exchange of energies, and there is a certain way that one should approach a prophet of God. We realize this at the doctor's office, beauty salon, grocery store, and other places, but it is a bit more difficult for us to understand when it comes down to financing God's prophet.

In religious financial appeals, many readily assume it to be a scam, failing to realize that abuse has existed in all arenas. There are attorneys, barbers, jewelers, and the list can go on and on of people who have initiated scams. In fact, there are many television commercials and products on the market that are no more than scams.

I become bothered by many people who desire to hear an accurate word from God, through my prophetic ability, but are appalled at giving money to do so. Now, for many years, I would share prophetic words with no thought of money. However, I soon began to realize how I was being taken advantage of.

There are many who feel that people with God-given gifts should perform those gifts without any charge. However, what about the persons who are gifted lawyers, or hair stylists, musicians and singers? Should all these people never charge for their services? Yet, if that's your perception, how do you expect Fred Hammond, Patti LaBelle, and others to live and care for their families? It must be realized they, too, have God-given talents. Even with yourself, God has given you an ability to be a good employee. Should you not be paid for your time and labor at your place of employment?

Approaching a Prophet

When it comes to prophetic ministry, there is a certain Biblical way to approach the prophet.

1 Samuel 9:3-10 states the following:

"And the asses of Kish Saul's father were lost. And Kish said to Saul his son, Take now one of the servants with thee, and arise, go seek the asses.

And he passed through mount Ephraim, and passed through the land of Shalisha, but they found them not: then they passed through the land of Shalim, and there they were not: and he passed through the land of the Benjamites, but they found them not.

And when they were come to the land of Zuph, Saul said to his servant that was with him, Come, and let us return; lest my father leave caring for the asses, and take thought for us.

And he said unto him, Behold now, there is in this city a man of God, and he is an honourable man; all that he saith cometh surely to pass: now let us go thither; peradventure he can shew us our way that we should go.

Then said Saul to his servant, But, behold, if we go, what shall we bring the man? for the bread is spent in our vessels, and there is not a present to bring to the man of God: what have we?

And the servant answered Saul again, and said, ***Behold, I have here at hand the fourth part of a shekel of silver: that will I give to the man of God, to tell us our way.***

(Beforetime in Israel, when a man went to enquire of God, thus he spake, Come, and let us go to the seer: for he that is now called a Prophet was beforetime called a Seer.)

Then said Saul to his servant, Well said; come, let us go. So they went unto the city where the man of God was."

When Saul lost his father's donkeys, his armorbearer suggested, "Why don't we go find the prophet Samuel, who can tell us where the donkeys are?" We also see before they approached the prophet, the first question was immediately, "How much money do we have to bring to God's vessel? This is implying Saul knew it to be proper protocol or procedure to bring a gift to the prophet before using of his ministry.

Saul clearly stated, "The amount of money we have is what will be given to Samuel in order for him to give us the prophetic word regarding the donkeys." We see this same procedure being done in 2 Kings 8:7-9:

> *"And Elisha came to Damascus; and Benhadad the king of Syria was sick; and it was told him, saying, The man of God is come hither.*
>
> *And the king said unto Hazael, Take a present in thine hand, and go, meet the man of God, and enquire of the LORD by him, saying, Shall I recover of this disease?*
>
> *So Hazael went to meet him, and took a present with him, even of every good thing of Damascus, forty camels' burden, and came and stood before him, and said, Thy son Benhadad king of Syria hath sent me to thee, saying, Shall I recover of this disease?"*

Give Your Best

It is clear when one approaches a prophet, especially a reputable one, one should always take his best gift to honor the God-spirit that is housed within the prophetic gift. In one of my services, I was praying and prophesying to individuals as they were giving their offerings. As every person placed their offering in my hand, I would tell them what I was hearing for their lives in my right ear.

This one lady came and placed her offering in my hand, and I spoke to her what I heard, which to me seemed quite generic. While I was holding her hand, waiting to hear more from God, I heard Him speak very firm to me, "Stop trying to hear what I am not saying!" Wow, it really caught me off guard.

While on the way home, I asked God why He didn't give me more to tell the lady? He responded, "She didn't give Me her best, thereby she doesn't believe Me for My best!"

It's All for God!

I had to realize, too, just as many other people, when one gives to the prophet, they are giving to God's representative.

One Thanksgiving, I was taking a woman, along with her five children, home from church service. As she got out of the car she said, "Wait, Pastor, I've got something to give you." I was shocked when I saw this woman step out of her small two-bedroom apartment carrying a huge turkey towards my car. While she was walking, I started shaking my head and telling the woman, "I don't need the turkey." However, she kept walking towards my navy-blue New Yorker, and by the time she opened my back door to place the turkey in the car, God spoke in my right ear.

He reprimanded me for my thoughts by saying, "This gift is not for you; it's for Me. You are just the beneficiary, but I am the recipient." I became quiet and submissive to the will of God, in order for this lady to receive the blessing she so desired from God by giving me the turkey. Certainly, she did experience a most wonderful Thanksgiving, and, not only that, a very prosperous Christmas for her and her children.

It is true: if one can release it, then they can receive it. I have had countless people give me beautiful things. In turn, they also received greater than what they gave to God's servant. Luke 6:38 declares, *"Give, and it shall be given unto you; good measure, pressed down, and shaken together, and running over, shall men give into your bosom. For with the same measure that ye mete withal it shall be measured to you again."*

The Gift to Prosper You

The prophet does have a major gift to understand issues of the future; but also, he has an ability to prosper whatever is given to him. In other words, when you give to the prophet, your gift unlocks the prophetic and prosperity ability housed within the prophet. This is illustrated in scripture when Elijah was sent by God to Zarepath and met a widow woman preparing to cook one last meal for her and her son. Then they would just wait for hunger to bring death in their lives. However, the prophet met them with some instructions that unlocked prophetic manifestation and great prosperity in 1 Kings 17:12-16.

> *"And she said, As the LORD thy God liveth, I have not a cake, but a handful of meal in a barrel, and a little oil in a cruse: and, behold, I am gathering two sticks, that I may go in and dress it for me and my son, that we may eat it, and die.*
>
> *And Elijah said unto her, Fear not; go and do as thou hast said: but make me thereof a little cake first, and bring it unto me, and after make for thee and for thy son.*

For thus saith the LORD God of Israel, The barrel of meal shall not waste, neither shall the cruse of oil fail, until the day that the LORD sendeth rain upon the earth.

And she went and did according to the saying of Elijah: and she, and he, and her house, did eat many days.

And the barrel of meal wasted not, neither did the cruse of oil fail, according to the word of the LORD, which he spake by Elijah."

It was after she gave the portion to the prophet that she miraculously received provision of food to last her the duration of the famine. When you give to the prophet, it's not only for them to live and maintain their daily needs, but also for you to live.

Therefore, when one approaches a prophet, they should approach them with a gift of their best. This is why many prophets now charge a fee for prophetic consultations, in order for both parties to be prospered. The prophet is being supported by your finances, and the hearer is connecting with a true power of prosperity.

That is, if you are connecting to a true prophet and not a con artist.

Money Equals Energy

Money is simply energy. I use this illustration in my seminars. If I were to ask you to babysit my children, you may say "yes" just to be nice, even if you really didn't want to. However, if I were to ask you to babysit my children and at the same time, I put a hundred dollar bill in your hand, I guarantee I'll get a quicker favorable response.

I have seen some of the calmest people really lose their cool the moment their employer has messed up their check. This is because they have tampered with their source of energy. When one doesn't have any money, one feels drained and forced to be on lockdown. You don't want to drive because you must save gas. You can't get a hamburger from the fast food place or go out to the party because you feel everyone is going to notice that you don't have any money.

Yet, when money enters your life it brings with it an energy. This is what happens even when you come before God's representative. That energy equips the prophet to minister to you effectively and causes you to be a supporter of his ability. Not only that, you, too become financially increased by tapping into his prophetic prosperity.

Especially when it comes to financial matters and people desire for me to prophesy change in their finances, I become very adamant about them giving their best offering first and then I will pray. This is because of the previous scriptural examples. I don't care who prophetically speaks in your life, when it comes to money, everything must be done according to scripture.

I remember when I didn't follow this procedure, and I prayed and prophesied to member of my church. She told me once the settlement would come in, then she would give her offering. I believed her and went against the procedure. This woman did receive the exact amount I told her, but she didn't live up to her promise. She not only didn't give her promised offering, she even left the church.

I heard from this lady several years later and she apologized. She informed me that because she didn't do what she promised, her financial gain didn't last very long. A family member became extremely ill, and she even lost her job. Giving according to scripture is a safeguard for both the prophet and the hearer.

Yet, I must also say again: you must be very selective whom you allow to prophesy into your life. Don't just give your finances to anybody. Listen to your heart and trust the God-spirit within yourself that you will connect with a true prophet and true prosperity!

CHAPTER 9

BEWARE OF THE FALSE PROPHET

"If light never shines in the midst of darkness, the world will *only* see darkness!" These were the words I heard God speak to me one day while driving in Houston. God had spoken to me some days before about being a prophet for His usage to the world. I was very grateful for the few experiences I had with the prophetic ministry, but it wasn't what I wanted to do in ministry. Can you believe it? I didn't even want to pastor a church.

I remember one day God was speaking to me about being a prophet and even a pastor. I was in attendance at a massive service with the platform filled with preachers. I was sitting in the audience and I told God, "Why don't you use some of those preachers up there and leave me alone!" All I wanted to do in church was direct the choir or work with the music ministry. I wanted to follow the steps of the late Dr. Mattie Moss Clark.

I really didn't want to be a prophet because of some things I had seen as a young minister working at a gospel radio station. You see, all the preachers who came into town to do revivals would buy radio time to promote the meeting. Therefore, I had a chance to see them behind the microphone doing their thing.

I saw and heard many that were truly concerned about the welfare of the listeners, however, I also had my fair share of those who were only concerned about the offering. These people would try to hype up the people and say things on the radio such as, "God is showing me some things about you, but I can't tell on the air." I would wonder why they couldn't tell them on the air, the person is anonymous. However, it was all a tactic just to get the person to the service in hopes that they would give an offering.

And you know what? It worked! However, I told God if I have to act that way in prophetic ministry, I don't care to do it. I have seen people operating in prophetic ministry telling the people anything for the purposes of gaining finances and superiority for manipulation of God's people. Such practices within the Body of Christ must stop and integrity must be brought back to the ministry of prophecy.

A True Prophet

A prophet is someone inspired to give an inspired message. In Hebrew, "nabi" is used for prophet, which means "to bubble forth, as from a fountain" or "to utter." Therefore, a prophet is one who has received an inspired message to be relayed to mankind.

Yet, the next question we encounter is "where does the inspiration for the message come from?" Automatically, we would assume that it would come from the throne of God; however, that's not always the case.

> *"Then the LORD said unto me, The prophets*
>
> *prophesy lies in my name: I sent them not, neither*
>
> *have I commanded them, neither spake unto them:*
>
> *they prophesy unto you a false vision and*
>
> *divination, and a thing of nought, and the deceit*

of their heart." Jeremiah 14:14

God spoke to Jeremiah about how there will be some prophets whose inspiration did not come from Him, but from "the deceit of their heart." Yes, these individuals may be receiving a message and they may be inspired to relay it; however, it was not inspired by God. These persons we refer to as FALSE PROPHETS.

Like many others, I thought of false prophets as those persons who claim they are Christ and even those who start little cults, like David Koresh, Jim Jones and others. Well, believe it or not, I have a greater respect for these persons than for the false prophets we have today. The same spirit or characteristics of these former false prophets still prevail today, yet in a more hidden form.

The only difference between Koresh, Jones and the false prophets of today is that the former were more open and blatant with what they did. They took control over the minds of the people, making them do whatever was requested of them, having several sexual encounters with men and women, whether married or not, and mainly causing people to fear them more than our loving God.

Today, we have this same spirit in operation within many of our churches. Pastors, prophets, and preachers alike are causing congregants to become fearful of them. We have ministers, both male and female, manipulating the Body of Christ physically, emotionally, financially, and even sexually.

Cover of Appearance

I remember in my earlier years, being a young preacher, I was watching a Christian telecast and a singer came on to sing who is one of my favorites. An older female preacher, who was very wise and mature in the Word of God, was watching the telecast with me. I was so very excited when they announced the singer on television and I was impressed with their attire, looking so glamorous, and I thought they sang better than I've ever heard them.

Once the singing was completed, I couldn't wait to hear the response of this woman of God who was watching with me. She simply walked away from the television and stated with disgust how the singer can sing so good but with no genuine concern for the audience! In other words, the singer performed well with skill, but with no presence of God's power.

Many times, we have people in ministry that can look the part and speak with beautiful words of sophistication, yet they are not of good intention. For this reason, we must be mindful of the cover of appearance. I know you've probably heard the old, true statement: "everything that shines ain't gold!"

> "Beware of false prophets, which come to you in sheep's clothing, but inwardly they are ravening wolves." Matthew 7:15

Oh, no, I don't have anything against looking or dressing nice. Some people even try to locate a false prophet by their style of dress. That wouldn't be a fair indication at all. One's chosen style of dress is not determined by their ministry, but rather their own personal taste in clothes. I'm like some other preachers that are just as sincere, who love to wear nice alligator shoes, diamonds, and even the finer luxuries of life.

I believe, as people in ministry, we should represent and exemplify the prosperity of God with the message that all can attain the same prosperity. Too many Christians are professing Christ and appearing ragged, as if we serve a broke Savior.

I've often stated that if my prosperity teaching doesn't work for me, why would it work for you? I must be a product of my own teaching.

Yet, beware of the false prophet who likes to look well and speak with great power, as with any other prophet, but lacks God's power. Yes, they want to impress you and not really bless you or empower you. We must be cautious and wonder, is this prophet here as a sheep or a wolf waiting for it's next victim?

I've seen some preachers who look well from the outside; but behind the stage, you'll find a whole different story. To aid in the appearance of looking good with new clothes, good instruments, fancy cars, and precious jewelry, sometimes they have gotten members of their following to purchase these items under their name. Why? Because the preacher has bad credit!

I've counseled several people with these horrendous stories about this sort of thing being carried on. Let me also say that I don't feel anything is wrong with a follower helping out a ministry with their credit or finances. I have had some beautiful people to do the same for me. Yet, it must come to some point when the preacher or prophet must help themselves. I know of one preacher who has had bad credit for over eight years, but repeatedly buying new clothes, shoes, purchasing more radio time, etc. With all the money being spent on those items, he could have paid a credit repair service to fix his credit status. I even met one preacher who couldn't put anything in his own name. In fact, his financial status was so bad, he couldn't even open a banking account with his name on it for the ministry.

Many of these types of male preachers find women who they can prey on to secure the items of the church through means of portraying a strong father figure or a seductive spirit before them. With the absence of so many fathers in a society, many women are just looking for a strong-willed man to look up to and to serve as a replacement for that missing father in their life. I even heard one preacher go so far as to tell one woman in efforts to keep her in his ministry that she reminded him of his mother who passed away. Oh, brother! I guess she wasn't the type to be his daughter, or girlfriend, so he had to use another approach!

I've even seen how many of these victims are currently devastated financially and emotionally. I know one precious lady who has lost her vehicle and property in efforts of giving large offerings and financially taking care of the "man of God!" Because he was aware of most of her financial dealings, when she would receive a large sum of money, he would eventually ask for a large donation in the service. One must inquire within, Is this offering really to empower me or for this preacher to maintain his cover of appearance?

"But, wait! This prophet performed great miracles and several of their prophecies came to pass." Yes, but even the appearance of miracles can be deceiving. Everyone realizes that we have attorneys everywhere these days. Some are good and some are bad, but they are still considered attorneys. Even some of the bad ones have won cases in court! It's the same in the prophetic ministry. Some prophets have had their predictions to come to pass; however, they still lack the true anointing of God.

Matthew 24:24 declares...

> *"For there shall arise false Christs, and false prophets, and shall shew great signs and wonders; insomuch that, if it were possible, they shall deceive the very elect."*

I have seen this on more than one occasion where a false prophet will gain the trust of the people through the manifestation of the prophecy and later use manipulating tactics to control the believers. Remember what Jesus said in Matthew 7:22,23:

> *"Many will say to me in that day, Lord, Lord, have we not prophesied in thy name? and in thy name have cast out devils? and in thy name done many wonderful works?*
>
> *And then will I profess unto them, I never knew you: depart from me, ye that work iniquity."*

Where's the Fruit?

Matthew 7:16 states, *"Ye shall know them by their fruits."* I once read this statement, which I have repeated several times: "Prophets should be known by their fruits, as opposed to their gifts!" In other words, a prophet should be known by what they produce consistently. What are the results of this prophet's ministry?

I've seen how several prophets change addresses almost every year or two and it's not because of God's instruction. Many prophets have to move frequently because they have used up their resources in that city. They have used the believers for every dime they could get and now must find a new territory. Sometimes a good investigation is required as to why this preacher left his previous city. What was his reputation like in that city?

I encountered one prophet who was always referring to his several churches in Chicago, Monroe and Dallas, only to find out none of these churches still exist! If you had thriving ministries in these areas, what happened that all of them are closed down?

I met one false prophet whom I allowed to preach in my church for a very lengthy meeting. Of course, this was before I realized he was false. I guess you can say this was my "college lesson" about false prophets being that I was a young pastor. This prophet all of a sudden had to leave the service late one night and drive to Dallas. He told me that some woman was throwing rocks and breaking the windows of his home in Dallas.

It appeared he was being victimized; however, I later came to realize that this was a woman he had conned into purchasing this home for himself and even started a relationship with her. This prophet didn't pay the mortgage and eventually stopped seeing her. So, really, this financially broke and broken-hearted woman was just reacting to her pain and embarrassment.

Oh, this was just the beginning! I later came to realize this prophet, who did have some prophecies to manifest and was a good speaker across the pulpit, had conned many women, even an older woman who traveled with him from Chicago who spent her life savings on him. I have yet to have a pastor to speak well of this prophet because the fruit of this prophet has been proven to be bitter and poisonous to the Body of Christ.

I'm not against large offerings, financing items

for religious leaders, or even dating, but one's inspiration or motive is what I'm concerned about. That includes the motive of the giver, but, especially the motive of the prophet. I'm not the least bit perfect, and I have many blemishes on my record. However, I realize that I, myself and every person should operate in integrity as opposed to iniquity.

Iniquity is hidden deceit. Integrity is exposed truth! Now, one may not like the exposed truth; however, we can certainly respect it. This is what separates a true and false prophet. With false prophets, they have a hidden motive, mainly selfish gain. A true prophet of integrity will expose to you the truth, without any hidden motive. I told someone, "If you bother my wife or children in a disrespectful manner, I just may cuss you out!" Well, I'm being honest! It is a person's motive which classifies them as "true" or "false."

> *"Beware of false prophets, which come to you in sheep's clothing, but inwardly they are ravening wolves.*
>
> *Ye shall know them by their fruits. Do men gather grapes of thorns, or figs of thistles?*

Even so every good tree bringeth forth good fruit; but a corrupt tree bringeth forth evil fruit.

A good tree cannot bring forth evil fruit, neither can a corrupt tree bring forth good fruit.

Every tree that bringeth not forth good fruit is hewn down, and cast into the fire.

Wherefore by their fruits ye shall know them.

Not every one that saith unto me, Lord, Lord, shall enter into the kingdom of heaven; but he that doeth the will of my Father which is in heaven.

Many will say to me in that day, Lord, Lord, have we not prophesied in thy name? and in thy name have cast out devils? and in thy name done many wonderful works?

And then will I profess unto them, I never knew you: depart from me, ye that work iniquity."

Matthew 7:15-23

As prophets of God, we should undoubtedly display "the fruit of the Spirit" as described in Galatians 5:22, 23:

> *"But the fruit of the Spirit is love, joy, peace, longsuffering, gentleness, goodness, faith, meekness, temperance: against such there is no law."*

When one comes in contact with a prophet, God's mouthpiece or representative, one should encounter a person who displays the characteristics of God. I've seen some prophets who present a message supposedly from God, but not in the character or tone of God.

I remember politely telling one of my sons, as I was ready to go to church, to go tell his brothers that it was time to go. Well, he went upstairs and yelled as if he was fussing: "Come on. Daddy's ready to go, NOW!" When he returned downstairs, I asked him why he said it like that: "Is that the way you heard me make the statement?" He responded, "No." He didn't know why he yelled the way he did. However, I wondered if it was because he felt as if because he was already dressed and ready to go, and felt proud of that fact, that he could fuss at his other brothers.

This is the way some prophets and persons in ministry are. We feel that we already have our lives together, or at least on the surface, therefore we can relay God's message with frustration or even disgust. I have heard some prophets speak with utter disrespect to the people of God. In services, they have stood people up and talked to them as if they were children being reprimanded. There are even prophets who will threaten to actually fight inside the church anyone who opposes them.

Is their behavior exemplifying the fruit of the Spirit or the personality of God? Is this preacher showcasing the love and temperance of God or the hostility of his own heart? One should always ask the question when encountering a prophet or any person of ministry, "Does this prophet illustrate the fruit of the Spirit, being God's mouthpiece or representative?"

No, not by any means does a prophet have to be perfect. Let's face it perfection is really a matter of opinion. We all know you can try so hard to be right, but there will always be someone who will find something wrong! Yet, in each religious leader, there should always be illustrated the character of God.

Just as one doesn't let everyone babysit their children, or not every beautician is allowed to care for one's hair, we need not to let everyone who claims to be a prophet speak into our lives without using our spiritual senses.

Listen, I'm all for helping and being a blessing to the prophetic ministry because there is a guaranteed blessing of increase for the giver. Yet, you must discern whether or not you are giving into a ministry of integrity. This can only be done by your instinct, which many people don't seem to trust. Yet, realize you have a spirit of God within yourself or some may call it your "conscience." However, learn to listen to it and see if your spirit, not your emotions, agrees with the spirit of the prophet.

"Beloved, believe not every spirit, but try the spirits whether they are of God: because many false prophets are gone out into the world."
1 John 4:1

Chapter 10

"Why Hasn't My Word of Prophecy Come to Pass?"

"And he said unto him, Behold now, there is in this city a man of God, and he is an honourable man; all that he saith cometh surely to pass: now let us go thither; peradventure he can shew us our way that we should go." 1 Samuel 9:6

"Are there any other prophets today like that of Samuel?" This was the tender question a dear pastor asked from Atlanta. He explained, and was somewhat dismayed, that not all prophecies were coming into manifestation, which was puzzling and many times downright frustrating.

Not trying to demean the prophetic ministry, but the question is one that deserves to be addressed: "Why don't all prophecies come true?"

It must be noted that many prophecies do come to manifestation, but what about those which do not? Those of us that are in the prophetic ministry already get quite a bit of ridicule because our ability from God is not always understood. Yet, to add to that, prophecies you've stated that didn't manifest puts the prophetic ministry in further embarrassment. There have been many times when I have been frustrated and felt I should quit the prophetic ministry because I was focusing on what did not happen.

However, one day God spoke to me to do the opposite, focus on the thousands of prophecies I've given that did come to pass. Truth be told, according to many scientists, critics and unbelievers, not one of the prophecies should ever manifest. So, the mere fact that many of the prophecies have come to pass is incredible by itself! The very truth that I'm able to sense information about people without knowing them is still pretty remarkable!

I remember in Dallas, Texas finishing my meal at a restaurant. I walked by this lady eating at a table with a young man. For some reason, God spoke in my right ear and told me to tell her that her family was going to be alright and they will find a new home. I didn't know this medium-sized white lady with dark, straggly hair who appeared to be in her late 30s. However, I went on and shared the word I heard for her family. She immediately looked at me with such shock and yet much sadness. She began to shake her head in amazement and asked me who I was. I told her who I was and that I am a prophet of God. She then became hesitant and gave me a question, which I knew was a test to see if I was really a prophet or a con man. She asked me, "How many children do I have?" I replied, "Six!" And she broke down in tears. She proceeded to tell me how she and her family just lost everything they had in a house fire!

Here's an incredible testimony submitted on my website:

> *"I would just like to thank you Prophet Mosley. You told me on the radio broadcast that there was someone close to me that had stomach problems. I*

told you that the person didn't live in Houston, which was my sister. I called her and asked her if she had pain in her stomach and she stated "no". You told me that this was serious. About 2 hours later, she began to experience excruciating pain from her stomach. She had gallstones, and one had come out of the pouch, which could have poisoned her system. She had the gallstones removed and is doing fine. I would like to just thank you for allowing God to use you. Continue to allow God to strengthen and bless you and your family."

-Penny

It is unmistakably true that many prophecies do come to pass. Yet, we must acknowledge the ones that don't. We must consider the single woman who was told she would get married in a year and still no husband after two years. Even the man looking for a better job and was told he would get one in 21 days and still didn't receive it. I even think about the person told they would get a house, and, yet, they remain in an apartment.

Many prophets have done their very best to avoid this one question. However, I felt in this book it would be a disservice to many who are trying to understand the prophetic ministry not to address such a popular and sincere question.

With this question remaining unanswered, it brings one to other questions:

- Was the prophet wrong?

- Was the prophet false?

- Does God not love me?

- Did I make God mad?

- Did I not do enough to acquire the blessing?

First, let's understand prophets are humans relaying God's heavenly message to His people. Therefore, the human side could make a mistake in its interpretations of God's message. So, bottom line, yes, the prophet could have been wrong!

That was one thing I was always afraid of - being wrong. However, there's nothing wrong with being wrong with right intentions. Remember, this is what separates the true and false prophet. As long as the prophet is not purposefully being wrong to manipulate you, each prophet should be given room for error. Let's face it! Everyone is going to be wrong at one point in time no matter what field one may operate in!

We must also remember that God's love is unconditional, which is very difficult for mankind to understand. For the most part, as humans, we love on the surface. If you make us mad, there are times when we will try our best to forget your existence!

Also remember that our loving God is sovereign. Simply put, He can do whatever He wants, including changing your prophetic manifestation. However, that change is not out of anger or you not being deserving, but, rather, done out of love for each person's overall development.

Sometimes, we're just not ready to receive that prophetic promise, either financially, emotionally, or even physically. Are you responsible enough with money to handle the promised $100,000 prophecy? Maybe there are still some emotional hurts from a previous relationship which you are not healed from that is keeping you from a new love. The reason your business has not prospered as prophesied could be because you need to be physically healthy to keep up with the late hours needed for a successful production. Everything and everyone involved with your prophetic manifestation must be in order. And sometimes everything is not in place as it should be.

I've even had men and women to come tell me how they are sure the person they have been dating is meant to be their spouse. Many of them even received prophetic words regarding that potential spouse. Yet, the potential spouse has not made a move towards marriage. What's up with that? Well, once again, everything and everyone must be in place for the prophecy to come to pass.

I shared with one gentleman, "God is not interested in forcing your potential mate to be with you. That wouldn't be a relationship based on love and free will. And because God has given you and I the ability to operate in free will, that potential spouse must come to that understanding of the feelings for you in order for the word to manifest."

Well, was that word wrong? No! I tell individuals, "According to your life right now, that prophecy is what is written in your file. Yet, if this individual doesn't desire to connect with you, then don't worry. God will adjust that file for you to find someone else compatible. However, that requires you being open to receive from God outside of what your heart has been set on." Oh, and, by the way, God is not going to give you less than your expectations! So, God is not going to take you from "wonderfully beautiful" to "horribly ugly!"

Remember, this same principle works with relationships, jobs, and even finances. Keep praying in expectation for your promised miracle! Don't ever give up, especially if you have sought counsel and confirmation for the validity of the prophecy. This is especially important! Get a confirmation from a reliable person who operates and understands prophetic ministry.

Before I was married, I received a call from a lady and she told me that God told her that I was her husband. While holding the phone in shock, I was trying to think of a way to help this lady without hurting her feelings. I assured the lady that God was possibly letting her know what type of husband she may marry however, I was not the actual person. You know after that conversation, I did tell the Lord it would be alright with me if He gave Janet Jackson that word! Of course, that's before I met and married the lady of my heart!

I have had people to contact me in tears wondering why their prophetic word hasn't come to pass. My heart feels their disappointment and frustration, yet, what word of comfort can I give them? One thing I say is to ask God: "What is hindering my word from fruition?"

It is almost as when Daniel was praying for an understanding of a vision, but his prayer was being blocked. However, he remained consistent in searching for the understanding of the vision. This is exactly how you and I must be when seeking the fulfillment of our prophecy!

> *"And he said unto me, O Daniel, a man greatly beloved, understand the words that I speak unto thee, and stand upright: for unto thee am I now sent. And when he had spoken this word unto me, I stood trembling.*

> *Then said he unto me, Fear not, Daniel: for from the first day that thou didst set thine heart to understand, and to chasten thyself before thy God, thy words were heard, and I am come for thy words.*
>
> *But the prince of the kingdom of Persia withstood me one and twenty days: but, lo, Michael, one of the chief princes, came to help me; and I remained there with the kings of Persia.*
>
> *Now I am come to make thee understand what shall befall thy people in the latter days: for yet the vision is for many days."* (Daniel 10:11-14)

I'm with you! I know one doesn't feel the desire to be persistent in prayer when it appears that nothing beneficial is happening. However, persistent prayer does work, and it lets God know how determined you are to receive what has been promised.

This chapter is strictly written to broaden your heart to be open to the possibilities from God as to why your word hasn't come to pass...yet! I have stated many possible reasons for the delay in your prophetic manifestation. Yet, the bottom line is as such: Many times, even with my ability to hear from God, I DON'T KNOW WHY YOUR PROPHECY HAS NOT HAPPENED!

Whew! That's really a challenge for many prophets to say! There are times when God will give a reason for someone's delay in receiving their prophetic manifestation. Then there are times when I just don't seem to get the reason for the delay. However, I do know that God is a loving God and will give you the ultimate of your desires and His promises if you continue to believe. *Jesus said unto him, "If thou canst believe, all things are possible to him that believeth." Mark 9:23*

I encourage you not to give up on your promise from God but seek to find the hindrance and pray directly for its removal. If you suffer from low self-esteem, that could be one reason for the delay in marriage. Then target your prayer to remove that low image of yourself and begin to take measures of action to enhance your own image. Maybe get a new wardrobe, get out and meet people at social events, or even lose a few pounds.

Okay, okay, that sentence was for me!

But, whatever you do, keep believing God!

CHAPTER 11

PROPHETIC COMMUNICATION

In seminars, I am often predicting...

- when a person should marry

- whether or not they are about to embark upon a good business deal

- the future for them and their children

- if they should move to another state

These are two questions I frequently receive: "How did you know that? How do you do what you do?" I remember I was just simply having a conversation with a man, and soon I started telling him things that he had not told me. He didn't know I was a prophet, but he became very uneasy with me. Becoming quite nervous, he asked me if I worked for the FBI. What a sigh of relief came over him when I told him I was a prophet!

Many prophets hear and perceive their messages from God in several different ways. The most common ways are through spiritual vision, hearing, feeling, smelling and tasting. Now, hold on for those of you that are in the church as I'm going to use some terms that many refer to as "psychic" or "metaphysical" terms. I use these terms because they simply identify the different methods of sensing God's message to the listeners. How can we say this word belongs over there and this word belongs in the church?

When I was really trying to understand my prophetic gift, I couldn't get any clear answers about prophesying. Many books I read just simply stated that the message just comes to you. I realized many of my prophetic colleagues were just afraid to use clear terms that describe the prophetic process perfectly.

Many people that are prophetic or intuitive receive their messages through clairvoyance (clear seeing), clairaudient (clear hearing), clairsentient (clear feeling), clairgustance or clairambience (clear tasting) and/or clairalience (clear smelling.)

Clairvoyance is the gift from God to be able to see pictures and mental images spiritually. This is what the Bible refers to as one being a "seer" (1 Samuel 9:9). This is one of my strongest methods of prophetic perception.

With clairvoyance, it works the same as if I told you to describe to me your home without you being there. One would immediately begin seeing that home in his mind's eye and start telling about the home's features. With clairvoyance, the prophet sees pictures within the mind's eye, which God reveals to him.

Once, while prophesying to someone in service, I kept seeing the face of my sister. It was almost driving me crazy as to why I kept seeing my sister's face while prophesying to this other lady, and my sister was nowhere in the service. Well, finally, I just asked the lady, "Do you know someone named Pamela, which is my sister's name?" She excitedly said, "That's my name!"

One gentleman came to me in a financial bind. He asked me to pray over some stock he was about to cash in on and wanted a miracle for the stock to be a tremendous financial relief for his family. As I held the paper in my hand, I saw in my mind's eye the paper tear right down the middle. I asked the gentleman, "Is there any way for this stock to split?" Now, I really didn't pay much attention in high school when we studied the stock market, and I don't know much about it now. The man replied, "There's no way with this type of stock." I told him, "I don't care what you say, this is what I see happening! Just call me 'crazy' and let me know what happens."

The next day, he came to me with a huge smile of his face and said, "I don't know how you do it, but you were right. Everything happened just like you said. The stock did split!"

Sometimes when I am praying for people, God will show me where they are ill. He may show me in a picture, but, mainly, I will see a red dot over the area of their body that needs healing. There are various ways that God may speak.

Clairaudience is the gift from God to be able to discern His divine message through internal hearing. I can't tell you how many friends I've had to tease me about my right ear. If you've ever seen me in a seminar or service, I'm sure you've heard me refer to hearing from God in my right ear. I've even had one friend to tease me when he calls and informs me to put the phone to my left ear so I can be sure to hear from God in my right ear.

Clairaudience works just like when you may hear a song on the radio earlier that day or even earlier during the week and the song keeps being heard within your head. In fact, there are times when I will be really stressing over an issue, and, from out of nowhere I will notice myself singing a song or hearing that song over and over in my head. That's when I realize, through the words of the melody, God is relaying a message of comfort to me.

On several occasions, people have come into my office or seminars with questions needing a prophetic answer. However, while they are asking me their question, I'm hearing God tell me about another issue they're having needing attention. So when they finish asking me their question, I'm responding with, "Yes, I heard you but what about the relationship with your brother, whom you haven't spoken to in years?"

One lady called during a live radio broadcast where I was prophesying to the callers. She called wanting to know about the success of her latest business venture. I listened to her and then asked why she wasn't preaching in church. This is what I heard in my right ear for the lady. She laughed and went on to say that others had told her the same thing and that she knew, undoubtedly, God must have told me!

While I was in Atlanta for a prophetic meeting, I was having lunch with a friend. In middle of eating my delicious baby back ribs, my right ear popped open and I heard God say, "Tell Sharon her mother is going to be okay. I'm going to be with her mother's left side." I quickly told Sharon what I heard. She looked back at me puzzled and didn't understand. I was puzzled too, but I knew what I had heard. I told her, "It may not make sense now, but just hold on to it."

She called me later that afternoon informing me she had called home to Florida to check on her mother. Her sister's response to her phone call was this: "You don't know what happened to Momma?" Sharon replied, "No, what happened?" Her sister preceded, "Momma just had a stroke on the left side of her body and was just admitted to the hospital!"

Another method of prophetic perception is clairsentience. This is the gift of God that allows people to actually feel the emotions and issues of others, and even God. Sometimes, when in meetings, I can tell when someone is really battling with asthma because my breathing will become very shallow.

I remember once praying for a lady; and while I was praying for her, my head began to hurt with great pain. I asked her, "Do you have a headache?" She asked me, "How did you know that? It's been bothering me for some days, and I'm going to the doctor tomorrow." I told her I could feel the pain. I prayed for her healing, which took place instantly, so she didn't need to keep her doctor's appointment.

Clairalience is the ability from God to be able to smell certain fragrances to receive a prophetic message. One very special lady in my church by the name of Sheila Welch, who has crossed over to be with the Lord, had this awesome ability. She had the wonderful ability to smell fragrances. She would often say, "Dr. Mosley, I smell a bouquet of flowers." And that is her message from God that something beautiful is about to transpire or that beauty is in the air. She can also smell evil, something rotten. Often, if there are evil intentions or motives in someone's heart, Sheila's senses allowed her to detect it through smell and odor.

Clairagustance, on the other hand, deals with taste. You've heard the expression "they left a bad taste in my mouth." Well, some people can literally do that. There are times when you will need chewing gum or a mint, and it won't be because of bad breath. You may be surrounded by ill will or evil intentions.

There are times when a sweet taste is left in my mouth. I am a lover of chocolate, and there are times when that taste will consume me, without my having eaten a thing. This is my cue that there is a "sweetness" about a person with a genuine heart.

These are just a few ways God will speak internally; but there are also external ways God will speak, not only to the prophet, but to anybody.

How is that you might ask? I shall never forget the time I was getting ready to conduct a seminar in Las Vegas, and I had to ask God if he really wanted me to go.

I felt the leading of the Lord through clairsentient. I felt it in my spirit.

I was driving along, and there was a van right in front of me. We were approaching a yellow light and the van slowed to a stop, rather than making it through the light. I'll be honest; I was fussing in my car because I felt we both could have made it through the light if he had gone on through. But, oh, well, I didn't realize God was trying to comfort my hesitation about Las Vegas.

Now, here I am in Texas, and when I looked down at the van's license, which was being held up by a plastic frame with most of it being torn off, that which was standing read "Las Vegas." It was staring smack-dead in my face. There are times when God will speak externally through signs, billboards, music, and, more importantly, the scripture.

Once when feeling despondent and lousy, I opened my Bible, for it to land on Hebrews 6:10, which I always keep in my memory.

> *"For God is not unrighteous to forget your work and labour of love, which ye have shewed toward his name, in that ye have*

ministered to the saints, and do minister."

I encourage you to be open to listen. When you hear that song on the radio about love and forgiveness, oftentimes, it is more than just a song. It is God trying to get a message through. God will speak to you in and through your situation. There are many ways to hear from God, but you have to be open and willing to allow him to communicate with you.

Once, I went to my computer to do some work and, of all days, it was inoperable and giving me major problems. I never believed for one minute that it was messing up on purpose; but I believe God was telling me, "Not now." Though I was frustrated because the computer kept shutting down, I still had clairsentient feelings, a feeling deep inside of me that God was trying to speak to me. I decided, through sheer frustration, to spend a little time with God in prayer. Later, I went back to use the computer, and it was working as if nothing had ever happened. Amazing, absolutely amazing!

Whatever it takes for God to get our undivided attention, he will do just that. There are no tricks or gimmicks; he simply wants to communicate with you and me. In the ministry of prophecy, there is no room for doubt, unbelief or what many may call "sheer coincidence."

Please, believe me nothing happens by just sheer coincidence. There is a reason for everything. We may not always realize or understand the reason, but there is always a reason. It may be years later when you realize, oh this is the reason why I met this person years ago or I kept this person's business card. It may not be for right now, but it's all a part of God's prophetic plan. Just keep allowing Him to communicate with you and allow the prophecies to unfold in your life.

CHAPTER 12

THE PROPHETIC MINISTRY... IN CHURCH!

Prophecy is communicating the thoughts and will of God to mankind. In most churches, especially that of a Pentecostal persuasion, prophecy has become a very essential part of the service. Most revival services of worship have an underlying expectation of a part of the service to include a form of prophecy.

Within the last decade, one can see the noun meaning of prophecy being replaced with the adjective of "prophetic." Our radio broadcasts, social media pages and emails have been inundated with flyers, announcements, commercials and messages related to prophetic conferences, prophetic prayer meetings, prophetic schools, prophetic worship services and the like.

"Prophecy...In Demand!"

This is an indicator that the ministry of prophecy is yet in demand and very attractive. People are still curious about the Will of God for their lives, or what the future has waiting for them or just the simple confirmation and assurance that God is yet noticing what the individual is experiencing in their immediate lives.

The usage of prophecy, forth-telling and foretelling of Spiritual matters, have been used in religious cultures such as Pentecostalism, Catholicism, Spiritual and Metaphysical movements. Prophecy has been used in many different modalities since the beginning of time which is inclusive of, but not limited to, personal readings, dream communication and interpretations, predictions, angelic communications, problem solving and much more.

It must be realized, whenever a person experiences any manifestation of prophecy, it is primarily "for edification [to promote their spiritual growth] and [speaks words of] encouragement [to uphold and advise them concerning the matters of God] and [speaks words of] consolation [to compassionately comfort them]." 1 Corinthians 4:13 AMP

"How Can I Say This...?"

Prophecy is not a new method of ministry or service from God to the world yet, it is a special gifting that is still in need of training and development that it may have an even greater impact on its recipients. Therefore, it must be understood, it's not merely the method of prophecy one uses (clairvoyance [hearing], clairaudience [seeing], etc.), or even the particular prophetic message being communicated. What is of greater importance in prophetic ministry is the HOW THE MESSAGE IS BEING COMMUNICATED.

What good is a message to be delivered if it is not served in a manner that is receptive? Prophetic messengers are to be representatives of God, showcasing his manners and characteristics of Love, since God is LOVE (1 John 4:8). One of the greatest problems I've witnessed in my years of viewing prophets and ministry of this kind, is the manner in which they give messages of prophecy.

While some messages have encouraged, excited and even comforted some people, there have been some messages that have discouraged, embarrassed, disgruntled and even drove people away from God, all because of the way the prophecy was given.

As prophetic ministers, it must always be in our minds that it's not what you say, but how you say it. Needless to say, there are times when a "tough" exterior is necessary, but it must always be accompanied by the unmistakable foundation of love, not hatred or even anger. Then there are the times when a gentle voice is needed to gently guide the more sensitive soul into the direction that caters to their betterment. (1 Kings 19:11, 12)

Let us examine some ways that Prophecy is NOT…

What Prophecy is Not…

1. *Prophecy is NOT* **Gossip but it is Gospel** – With the invasion of social media and news of triumphs and sorrows of everyday life, prophetic ministry must be sure to judge any message coming forth to be one initiated by divine intervention and not simply empathy or other emotions from personal hearsay.

> *"Besides that, they learn to be idlers, going about from house to house, and not only idlers, but also gossips and busybodies, saying what they should not."* 1 Timothy 5:13 ESV

2. ***Prophecy is NOT* Degrading but Uplifting** – It's been stated before, "you can get more bees with honey, than vinegar." Prophecy is to uplift the recipient and not cause them to feel worse. A prophetic messenger should never try to make the listener feel belittled to simply to enhance the prophetic messenger's ego. Therefore, it could also be stated that prophecy is not selfish, but sensitive!

> *A soft answer turns away wrath, but a harsh word stirs up anger. Proverbs 15:1 ESV*

3. ***Prophecy is NOT* Embarrassing but it is Empowering** – Many messages often disclosed to prophetic messengers are very private and personal. Prophetic messengers should feel honored that God trusts you to reveal sensitive matters about His children.

Therefore, delivering these messages must be handled with tack, sensitivity and caution.

> *"And the King will answer them, 'Truly, I say to you, as you did it to one of the least of these my brothers, you did it to me.'" Matthew 25:40 ESV*

4.   *Prophecy is NOT* **Concrete, but it is Conditional** – Although the divine message is given from the Universal presence of God, it can be altered. Many messages given in Biblical times were conditional and not necessarily concrete. As a rule of thumb, I encourage participants to know the message I'm hearing is based upon one's status or path in God as of right now. Depending on the situation, if you alter your path you can alter the results of your prophetic message.

> *"If my people who are called by my name humble themselves and pray and seek my face and turn from their wicked ways, then I will hear from heaven and will forgive their sin and heal their land." 2 Chronicles 7:14 ESV*

5. *Prophecy is NOT* **Authoritative, but it is Accompanying** – Prophets must be recognized as representatives of God and not God himself. The messages given must be spiritually discern as to how to be delivered and should serve as an accompaniment to God's Biblical and overall message of LOVE.

> *"Rather, speaking the truth in love, we are to grow up in every way into him who is the head, into Christ." Ephesians 4:15 ESV*

6. *Prophecy is NOT* **Guessing but it is Assuring** – With the demand and desire of many to hear a comforting prophetic message, at no time must a prophecy be one of guessing or lying. No prophet is required to know all the answers to the questions being asked. In fact, it gives more credibility to the messenger to convey to the participant what God in NOT revealing, assuring the participant you are really concerned with giving accurate information.

> *"Do not be anxious about anything, but in everything by prayer and supplication with*

thanksgiving let your requests be made known to God." Philippians 4:6 ESV

"For now we see in a mirror dimly, but then face to face. Now I know in part; then I shall know fully, even as I have been fully known." 1 Corinthians 13:12 ESV

7. **Prophecy is NOT Judging but it is Guiding** – Every prophetic minister should be able to put aside their personal convictions, emotions, judgments and opinions when delivering a prophetic message. It must be remembered we are trusted to be the messenger delivering the message without personal opinions. Messages should not be merely, or even ever be, a reflection of religious doctrine or beliefs but that of the guidance of God for the recipient.

"And he said to them, "You yourselves know how unlawful it is for a Jew to associate with or to visit anyone of another nation, but God has shown me that I should not call any person common or unclean." Acts 10:28 ESV

8. ***Prophecy is NOT Unjustly Attacking but it is Ultimately Affirming*** – The Prophet has been given great authority to command spiritual happenings, including blessings and curses. Yet, with this tremendous power, one must be very cautious not to abuse this divine power. Although these occurrences brought forth much respect and affirmation to the power of God and the divine power of the prophet, one must never just speak an attacking word to anyone unjustified. A prophet's words and actions carry great weight and must be respected at all times. Yet, the prophet must treat everyone with respect.

> *"But whoever causes one of these little ones who believe in me to sin, it would be better for him to have a great millstone fastened around his neck and to be drowned in the depth of the sea."*
> *Matthew 18:6 ESV*

TESTIMONIALS

These are just a few of the many testimonies given by some precious people. I certainly thank all of these persons and others who have written, e-mailed and verbally shared their testimonies with me. Please, be assured it is this chapter of the book that I will read the most! Often, I have referred back to the many testimonies from people across the country, which I keep in my desk when I need encouragement.

Thank you to all of you who have allowed me to share my gift from God with you. I love you dearly!

"Michael Mosley is a 'sho' nuff seer'! His first prophecy to me was when I was visiting his church in Houston. He stated that someone was going to financially bless me very quickly and very soon. About a week later, I was visiting a church in New York and a nationally-known preacher recognized me and asked to speak with me after the service. It was then this precious woman of God wrote me out a check for $6000 as a gift for me!

Apostle Mosley also prophesied to me at another time about a house in Florida I was to acquire. He described the house and even stated that there was some water in the back of the house. Just a few months later I acquired the exact home with a pool and a lake in the back of the house!

This man of God and I have become great friends and have traveled together. He has been a tremendous blessing to my church and my life. He is really a true prophet of God."
Rev. Gail
Orlando, Florida

"Prophet Michael Mosley is one of the greatest men of God I know! We consider him as our resident prophet of our church. During a crucial time in our ministry, we were being threatened to be put out of our church facility.

Prophet Mosley said that we would hear good news on a certain date. Up until that time, our financial institution did not even want to talk with us for any further negotiations. However, on that exact date, our church received word that the bank was ready to renegotiate our deal.

Prophet Mosley also stated during a visit to church that we would not lose our building. He went further to state that everything was already worked out and we were not to move. A few weeks after his visit to our church, everything worked out just as he stated. God even amazed us more when the bank forgave half-a-million dollars of our debt. This man certainly hears from God and walks with God!"

Dr. James
Greensboro, North Carolina

"Some people can only hear an echo from God, but Michael L. Mosley hears the voice of God! While ministering in my church, he told me that God was opening a quick door for me to be on television and he stated that he saw me on Trinity Broadcasting Network. At the time, I had no idea how that prophecy was going to manifest.

In a matter of weeks, I received a surprise call from TBN asking me to appear on the network, not locally, but nationwide, for an interview with Dr. Juanita Bynum. God has given Prophet Michael Mosley a unique gift, and I value the anointing that he carries from God."

Prophet Darryl, Pastor
Atlanta Georgia

"Prophet Michael Mosley is a real prophet of God. I've called him on a few occasions to hear the word God has for my life. I don't allow everyone to speak into my life, but he is one that I know is sent by God and used mightily by the Lord."

Shundra
National Gospel Recording Artist

"My wife and I know that the word of prophecy given by Michael Mosley was true. He spoke of a loan and that we were turned down for it. Well, at that moment I didn't remember. However, it was my wife that had previously applied and was turned down. But a week after hearing his prophecy of going back and applying again for the loan, we did it and were approved. My wife and I thank

God for the phenomenal ministry of Michael Mosley!"
Bryant
Miami, FL

"Prophet Mosley told me that I was to receive a financial increase that would cause my finances to be multiplied. He further stated that this was dealing with my job in real estate and this increase was to happen around December 7th and 14th.

I can't tell you how surprised I was when someone called me unexpectedly on December 7th and informed me that I have been awarded a special key for outstanding service in real estate. To my amazement this key was to unlock a special box with a minimum of $50,000! Not only that, but I was to unlock the box during a special Christmas banquet on December 14th! To God Be the Glory! Prophet Mosley, thanks for letting God use you. You really are an inspiration to many people."
Kathy
Chicago, Illinois

"Dr. Mosley prophesied to me about my fall semester in college. I planted a $1000 gift into his ministry. He told me I was going to receive finances and I should take care of all my needs and expenses with the monies I'd be receiving. Prior to that prophecy, he told me that some monies were being held up in financial aid department that I didn't even know about.

Well, I had an appointment with a supervisor in the financial aid department regarding some grant money that I recently found out had been held up from last semester because of an administration error. At first, he wanted me to wait until the next day so that he could get a possible approval from his director. With that, there was a 50-50 chance of me getting the money, based on the decision of the director.

But before I left the office, not only did he give me the $1500 from last semester, but he gave me an additional FREE $1600 (not a loan) AND changed the loan I already had to one of a much lower interest rate that will never increase. You are truly a man of God!"
Nancy
Houston, Texas

"The first time I'd ever attended one of Michael Mosley's classes or even met him, for that matter, was an intriguing and surprising experience. I had no idea of what to expect and I just went with an opened mind. The very first thing he said to me was this: 'You've been searching for employment; you are looking for a job. God wants you to know that you will have a job very soon. You will be hired by someone that you have already spoken with, by someone that already has your resume.'

By now, I was very intrigued and thinking to myself, I've only had two interviews, and I've received exactly two rejection letters from both companies. I admitted to him that I was searching for employment and had been for several weeks, but I said nothing about my two rejection notices. Michael then went on to speak of several other past and current aspects of my life. All were fascinating and accurate. He even said, directly to me, 'You cut your own hair today.' That statement alone was the absolute affirmation for me! I was completely alone while I trimmed my own hair over the bathroom sink that very morning, and I never mentioned it to another living soul until that moment.

Several days after my meeting with Michael, I received a phone call from one of the companies that had given me a rejection letter. The person that they'd hired for the job didn't work out. They wanted me to start immediately and I am still there today...with a smile on my face and in my heart."

Robin
Houston, TX

"God bless you man of God, Apostle Mosley.
I have seen and heard some prophets in my time, but none quite as accurate as I heard from you.

I have to tell you, in the beginning I was very skeptical about you because the people that say they are prophets/prophetesses aren't what they say, and they'll only help you or pray for you if it benefits them; but I find no fault in you."

Catrina
Lake City, South Carolina

"Dr. Mosley prophesied in February that I was getting married really soon. I wasn't even in a relationship with anyone at the time. However, I praise God that I met the most wonderful man; he loves Jesus and is a worker with me in the church. We married four months after that prophecy was given. Wow! Thanks for giving me hope, Apostle. My husband and I really thank God for your ministry!"

Mrs. Jackson
Las Vegas, Nevada

"The ministry of Dr. Michael Mosley is simply phenomenal. He is a chosen mouthpiece for God. Every time he comes to our city, I encourage the people to come and hear such an accurate and empowered vessel of God. He has blessed my life and ministry in numerous ways. He has been a great help to many in the city of Las Vegas.

He prophesied that my church would be featured in a magazine. Shortly thereafter, a national magazine asked me if they could do a story on our church! Apostle Mosley also spoke that I would be featured on television. Well, again, I was asked to participate in a television program here in the city! Without a doubt, Apostle Mosley is a truly wonderful gift, not just to the body of

Christ, but unto mankind!"

Dr. Anne, Pastor
Las Vegas, Nevada

"I attended a service in Galveston, Texas where Michael Mosley was speaking. He asked if I was trying to get pregnant and I said, 'Yes.' My mother-in-law, Grace, was with me and he asked her if she had lost a child. Indeed, she had many years ago. He went back to me and said, 'If you had a child you would already know the baby's name.' (In thinking, if I was going to have a boy, it was going to be named after my husband, Eric.)

Michael also stated that something in the back of the house need to be repaired. I told him that weeks before, the patio between our detached garage and kitchen had collapsed. He said, 'Okay – it's you! You are related to her how?' (pointing to my mother-in-law) It was then I revealed how we were related. He then told me that I would be holding my child by this Christmas.

He also stated, I would be receiving some money in the month of April. Lightheartedly, I said, 'Yeah I know - income tax.' He said, 'No, not income tax.' Fact: In

March we received our income-tax return, not in April.

Well, my husband, (who was not at that service with Michael and knew nothing of what he stated) along with myself, decided to adopt a child and the process went very quickly. Eric and I had about 6 weeks to contact a lawyer and arrange the finances. Eric and I received the money to pay for the adoption in APRIL! When we learned the baby might be a girl, Eric's exact words were this: 'I already know the baby's name.' He said he wanted it to be 'Wendy.' The name of his sister - the name of the child my mother-in-law lost!
Happy ending: By Christmas, I was holding my child."
Elena
Texas City, Texas

"I met Dr. Mosley via telephone, another pastor placed him on a three-way call with me. Upon our introduction, one of the first things Apostle Mosley stated to me was, "Don't let go of the television ministry!"

I didn't even have a chance to tell him what my concerns were or even the fact that I was on television. However, he picked it up in the Spirit, that the television ministry

was one of my greatest concerns at that time. On top of that, I had to have this powerful man of God to visit our church and God gave our church, one of the greatest revivals we've ever experienced!"
Dr. David
Shreveport, Louisiana

"I first met this man of God via telephone. One of my members was attending a service he conducted in the Atlanta area. While on the phone, Dr. Mosley told me to have some people praying for me. He saw me having an accident or a problem with my leg. I remember just jotting down the words of the prophet and simply thanking him for what God had revealed to him.

A few weeks later, I slipped and fell down the stairs and fractured my leg. While in excruciating pain, I thought, "This was what the prophet was talking about." I knew then this man was really sent of God. He has been a great blessing to my church, family and ministry."
Pastor D
Atlanta, Georgia

"During a Saturday prophetic service, Dr. Mosley looked at me and told me I would be driving another car really soon. I just received the word; but, at the time, I wasn't looking to purchase another vehicle. However, by that following Friday I was driving a new vehicle.

I took my car in to be serviced and, while waiting, the salesman took me to look at some new cars. My current car was in excellent condition and I loved it; and, anyway, I knew to purchase another car now, I would be upside down on the trade in. However, this salesman told me to choose something I liked, and he'd take care of the rest. I did just what he stated. Not only was I approved, but my car was allowed to be traded-in, and my notes were less than what I was paying previously. I'm so appreciative of the prophet. I don't know if I would have had the courage to go for the new car if he hadn't spoken it into my life!"

Patricia,
Rocky Mount, North Carolina

Hey Dr. Mosley!!!!
Just wanted to update you...we went ahead and looked at some other houses....we found a house that is in an awesome neighborhood, zoned to the schools we wanted

and a wonderful backyard. The owner didn't even check our credit or background, you said that by my mom and step-daughter's birthday, that the house would be handled. Well, their birthday is Monday, and we put the deposit down on the house yesterday!!! We are really excited....
Love and light...
Rachell
Houston, TX

In one of his meetings, Prophet Mosley spoke to me and mentioned that I had a brother that needed immediate medical attention. I told him that I did have a brother in California, however I didn't believe he was sick. Michael was very persistent that I would give him a call and have him to visit the doctor. I called my brother and he did tell me that he wasn't feeling well but didn't know what was wrong. He went to the doctors and immediately the doctors performed a triple bypass surgery on my brother. The doctors told my brother if he would have waited any longer, he wouldn't be alive. Thanks Prophet Mosley for saving my brother's life!
Faye
Houston, TX

Dr. Mosley, I truly thank God for your gift! You may not remember this, but you spoke to me when you were on stage at a concert a few years ago in Houston. I don't know how you could see me up in the balcony, but you described what I had on and told me that God was going to replace my truck! I was shocked because I knew you didn't know that I had just lost my truck. In about two weeks, I had another truck brand new! I had never met you, but I will never forget you. I found you on Facebook and I had to share my testimony. Keep doing what you're doing! You are a man of God!
David C.

About the Author

Along with being an Intuitive Life Coach and a Certified Clinical Hypnotherapist, Dr. Michael L. Mosley has been labeled by his peers as one of America's Premier Prophets and one of the most innovative Spiritual Teachers of our time! He has shared his teachings and prophetic insights with thousands via radio, television, conferences, and seminars. For over 25 years, He has inspired the lives of many, including pastors, professional and political leaders! His keen abilities have afforded him to be featured around the country and internationally through his syndicated radio program, *"Your Spiritual GPS to Success!"*

Dr. Mosley currently resides in Atlanta, Georgia with his wife, Annilia Wright-Mosley, and enjoys being a father to his six children. In the midst of In the midst of much traveling, speaking, lecturing, pastoring, and giving private consultations, Dr. Mosley remains an avid student of Spiritual Truths!

Connect with Dr. Michael L. Mosley

Spiritual Teacher, Prophet, Intuitive Life Coach

★ *Address: 950 Eagle's Landing Pkwy, Suite #434 Stockbridge, GA 30281*

★ *Website:* www.drmichaelmosley.com

★ Phone: 916-467-4448

Schedule your private reading today, text *"reading"* to "40691"

Share some of your favorite quotes or portions of this book via social media by tagging Dr. Mosley and using the following hashtags: **#DrMLM** or **#ProphMLM**

Twitter: @drmlmosley

Facebook: Dr. Michael L. Mosley

Linkedin: Dr. Michael L. Mosley

Email: office@drmichaelmosley.com

Stock images above used with license permissible by Google images, 2018 and are used for illustrative purposes only.

www.ingramcontent.com/pod-product-compliance
Lightning Source LLC
Chambersburg PA
CBHW070453100426
42743CB00010B/1607